CHINESE CHRISTIAN THEORIA

華人基督徒雜談

ONE MAN'S CONTEMPLATIONS ON FAITH AND THE CHINESE CHRISTIAN MISSIONARY

一個基督徒對信仰及在華傳教士的省思

Joel C. Kwok, Ph.D.

郭志豪博士

Translations By
中文翻譯

Reverend Grace L. Song
宋靈光牧師

For God's Glory.

Grace

DOVE'S HERALD PUBLISHING
San Francisco, California

A DOVE'S HERALD PUBLICATION

First Edition, Copyright © 2013, Joel C. Kwok

Printed in the United States of America.

Cover Photograph: "Svartsengi" © 1991 Lance Chang (changstudio.com).

Scripture quoted herein are taken from *The Holy Bible, New International Version.*

ISBN: 978-1-304-55692-9 (Hardcover)
ISBN: 978-1-304-55681-3 (Paperback)

We stand on the shoulders of missionary giants
for a try at grasping their horizon.
We can only emulate them—
to become better followers, knowing:

"HE IS NO FOOL WHO GIVES
WHAT HE CANNOT KEEP TO GAIN
THAT WHICH HE CANNOT LOSE."

Inspired by Jim Elliot and Eric Liddell

Joel C. Kwok, Ph.D.

CHINESE CHRISTIAN THEORIA

ONE MAN'S CONTEMPLATIONS ON FAITH AND THE CHINESE CHRISTIAN MISSIONARY

Chinese Translation by

Rev. Grace L. Song

郭志豪博士

華人基督徒雜談

一個基督徒對信仰及在華傳教士的省思

中文翻譯
宋靈光牧師

Contents

Bamboo Inside
© Lance Chang, 2006
CHANG STUDIO, changstudio.com

Introduction

Chinese American congregations in the United States have grown exponentially in the last decade, with a predominant number of sermons held bilingually. Also, while Christian missions to China date back to the Tang Dynasty in the 8th century, the growth of Chinese Christians has been particularly significant in the last 40 years. I write this book with these developments in mind and hope my book will both supplement bilingual congregations and facilitate Christian dialogue between English and Chinese speakers. The purpose of these essays is to enrich Bible discussions at fellowship gatherings, inspire conversation about the topics herein, or to liven up a sermon.

The heritage of this collection began humbly with the monthly newsletter published at my church. Like most church members, it was my habit to pick up the monthly newsletter circular, peruse it lightly, note a few social news or church events, and then most of the time, leave the newsletter on the same table I found it on. One day it occurred to me that this pamphlet held so much potential. It could be used as one more channel of communication for possible enlightenment that to date had not been optimally used. If such a newsletter contained articles that prompted me to think deeper about my faith, then I would take that newsletter home with me.

Thus began my diligent authorship of articles for the Sunday newsletters. As it is with many Chinese American Christians, the congregation I attended was bilingual, and so I was conscientious about presenting the faith articles in both English and Chinese. The articles proved successful. Readers would come to me and email me to discuss the topics presented in these newsletters and Christian dialogue even extended to Hong Kong and China, much farther than the church walls.

The topics presented herein are from my personal contemplations on faith and the Bible as one who was trained in science, with a particular emphasis on the Chinese Christian mission and aspects of Christian history that would be interesting to a person of Chinese orientation. I hope such a focused collection will be most relevant to Chinese American congregations or Christians in China who seek religious texts that will resonate directly with them.

If my little collection of articles on faith and the Chinese Christian mission can inspire one church member to spearhead deeper faith articles in his or her congregation newsletter, to continue the work of writing about faith at the intersection of the Chinese or Chinese American culture, then my book will have been a great success to me. I encourage congregations to republish any of the articles herein or integrate these topics into fellowship discussions or sermons. I hope they will provide great prompts for deepening and broadening our faith and the knowledge of Christianity.

I wish to express gratitude to my dear friend, Sunny Woan, Esq. for her invaluable input in the publishing process. She found time in her very busy law practice to make the publication of this book possible through her excellent and effective editing and organization, without which this book would not have been completed. Words cannot express my gratitude for her sympathy with this project.

Reverend Grace L. Song deserves immeasurable credit for the translations into Chinese. Rightfully, Reverend Song should be listed as a co-author, but her modest, unpretentious spirit has declined such credit. Nonetheless, her contributions must be recognized. Miss Susan Hon, a fellow Christian serving her mission in Guangzhou, China, has also contributed significantly to the fine-tuning of the Chinese text. I owe deepest gratitude to both Reverend Song and Miss Hon.

Joel Kwok

引言

過去十年，講中英雙語的華人教會在美國不斷增長。此外，自基督教於8世紀的唐朝進入中國之後，華人基督徒的增長於過去40年尤其顯著----此書寫作過程中，這些發展影響著我的思路。

此書目的是為了促進基督徒中英雙語間的對話，豐富雙語教會團契聚會的討論，啟發對本書各主題的反省，甚至增添講道的趣味。

此著述構思始於本人所在教會的月報。與多數會友一樣，本人已習慣於信手拈起教會月報、稍作瀏覽、一掃社交消息或教會大事，之後隨手將其置於舊有的月報當中。直到有一天發現，手中的月報其實頗具潛能，既可多方啟蒙、又能彼此溝通，祇可惜未能善加利用。月報所載錄的文章，若能夠令人深刻反省一己信仰，我會愛不釋手。

由此，我開始勤奮地為教會月報撰寫文章。教會會友多操雙語，故所有有關信仰的文章皆由英中文書寫，而文章被證實是成功的。很多人前來與我討論文章的內容，討論與對話甚至跨越教堂的牆壁，延及香港及中國大陸。

本書著述，乃本人由一個科學家的角度，發表對信仰及聖經的思考。所注重的華人基督徒使命，及中國基督教歷史的層面，對俱中國背景的人則是一个有趣指引。本人希望此書能夠在尋求信仰的美國華人及中國基督徒中間產生共鳴。

此討論信心與中國基督教使命的拙作，若能夠激發即使一位教會成員，於其所在教會繼續撰寫關於信仰的文章，討論有關中美文化間更深層面的信仰話題，此書對我來說已獲相當的成功。本人鼓勵各位使用和發佈本書文章，並將其議題納入團契討論甚至教會講道。甚願本書為深化和擴大我們對信仰及基督教的了解，提供良好的推動。

在出版過程中,温善铃律師為本書提供了無比寶貴的意見，言語無法表達本人的感激之情。在無比繁忙的律師生涯中，她出色有效的編輯與組織技能令本書得以完善。離開温女士的熱情及俠義之心，此書出版無望。

宋靈光牧師將本書翻譯成中文，功不可沒。誠然，宋牧師應列為共同作者，但她謙卑地婉拒此譽。儘管如此，她的貢獻仍須獲得承認。

於中國大陸服侍青年基督徒的韓俏文女士，與本人素未謀面，卻為本書中文部分的潤色提供了慷慨的幫助，本人為此銘感於心。

郭志豪

THE CHINESE CHRISTIAN MISSION

華人基督徒之使命

The Chosen People Were Not the First People

The Judeo-Christian heritage has such a strong influence in Western civilization that we sometimes subconsciously think of the Jewish as one of the first peoples to walk the earth if not the first. I want to dispel this notion with no disrespect. It may be my own blind spot that I wish to correct, but I hope my rummage through history and prehistory gives you some diversion. For some beginning students of the Bible, it is not inconceivable that Adam and Eve might be mistaken for Jews. Of course, we know that Jews as a chosen people did not come about until Abraham, around 1800 B.C.

Much happened before that and we would be wise to guard against wrong assumptions concerning the age of Israel's origins. The second millennium B.C. is nowhere near the dawn of time. Archaeologists have discovered earlier cultures in Egypt, Syria, Palestine, and Mesopotamia which predated Abraham by several millennia. For the sake of comparison, Abraham lived during the time of the Chinese Xia dynasty, the legendary first dynasty of China. The Chinese race certainly originated long before the dynasty.

The last ice age almost wiped out the human race, save for some survivors in a small corner of Africa. In the ninth century B.C., man was able to take the first step toward a food-producing economy. Around 8000 B.C., the cave-dwelling Natufian culture of Palestine learned to harvest grain. Jericho was a Neolithic village in the seventh or sixth millennium B.C., no longer a cave-dwelling culture. Similar villages existed in Phoenicia (today's Lebanon), Syria, and Mesopotamia. Not to be forgotten was Egypt, and all this happened more than 2500 years before Abraham.

No one knows where the first people to create civilization in Mesopotamia came from. They were the Sumerians who left inscriptions among the relics of Ur, the city of Abraham's father. The Sumerians were not the only people dwelling in Mesopotamia. There were some Semites, descendants of Shem, known as Akkadians, who adopted the Sumerian pantheon of gods. These Semites eventually established the Empire of Akkad about 2360-2180 B.C., near Babylon. In time, Sumerians and Semites mixed completely. Israel was born into a melting pot that was already ancient.

The essence of the Israelites was not being first, but being chosen. We are the new Israelites and we have been chosen.

選民未必是第一個民族

眾所周知，猶太基督教文化遺產在西方文明中有舉足輕重的影響，因此，每逢提及猶太人，很多人下意識地以為他們即是人類歷史上首個粉墨登場的族類。

這種說法有待商榷、校正。或者這曾是我個人的盲點，但透過翻抄史前史，希望能夠引發你對選民歷史的興趣。

某些初讀聖經的人,以為亞當夏娃都是猶太人。其實，許多歷史事件的發生早於亞伯拉罕的年代，公元前1800年亞伯拉罕之后，猶太人才成為一個民族，成為神的選民，所以，不要先入為主的假設以色列人是最原始的族群。

遠遠后期於地球開始的主前第二個千年，考古學家在埃及、敘利亞、和米索布達米亞所發掘的遠古文化，就已早於亞伯拉罕之前的許多個千年。如若比較，亞伯拉罕的年代與傳說中中國的夏朝同期，但中國各族於夏朝之前早已存在。

冰河時代結束於萬年之前，那時除了非洲的某個角落之外，人類的足跡幾乎湮沒。公元前八千年人類開始種植谷物，到公元前六至七千年，耶利哥脫離山洞文化，成為新石器時代的村落，類似的村落也出現在腓尼基（即今日的黎巴嫩）、敘利亞、和米索布達米亞，當然包括埃及，這些大約發生於亞伯拉罕之前的二千五百年。

我們無從知道米索布達米亞第一個發明文化的蘇米利安民族由何而來。這個民族古老的文字曾遺留在亞伯拉罕的故鄉吾耳。不僅蘇美利安人居住於米索布達米亞，閃的后裔同樣在那裡居住，並組成自己的王國，稱之為押甲族。公元前2360～2180年，他們與蘇美利安人混合，群聚與巴比倫。

在這個多元融合的背景中，以色列誕生了。

Christian Entry in China

The very early contacts between China and Christianity date back to the Tang dynasty (7th century AD) and again to the Yuen dynasty (13th century AD). Only archaeological remains testify to those encounters. Further exchanges had to wait until the Portuguese sailed to Asia in the 15th century AD.

Missionary work in these times was the efforts of the Roman Church. Francis Xavier labored in India and Japan before attempting to enter China. Sadly, he died within sight of the China coast in 1552.

The Portuguese traders carved out for themselves a small colonial enclave, Macao, on the China coast about sixty miles from the major trading city of Canton. It is the same Macao that is famous for its Las Vegas ambiance today. It was intended to be the missionary center for China, but the Chinese dynasty, Ming, forbade entry into China proper. The missionary work stagnated on account of colonial interference and a lack of sensitivity to cultural differences. It took the combined wisdom of three brilliant and inspired individuals to make the first entry. Ricci, Ruggieri, and Valignano refuted the idea that the Chinese language was impossible to learn, and they did away with the idea that Chinese converts had to adopt western dress. This principle of cultural accommodation or adaptation became the hallmark of Jesuit missions.

Ruggieri found a key to win the attention of the Chinese authority by demonstrating knowledge of western technology in which the Chinese showed great interest. He gave a watch to a general of the army. It was a sensation. He and Ricci were allowed to live in China. Ricci, in God's providence, was the ideal man for China, with a prodigious memory, and a sound knowledge of mathematics, astronomy, and cartography. He astounded Chinese scholars with a map of the world and the idea that China might not be the only center of the world. Just as significant, he proved to be a master linguist. He learned the Chinese language and memorized much of the Chinese classics and could write hundreds of Chinese characters. It was most impressive.

Mateo Ricci was eventually to become the most famous missionary in China. His experience and wisdom convinced him that the best hope for the Christian message lay with capturing the attention of the emperor. His reputation persuaded a provincial governor to take him to Beijing to celebrate the emperor's birthday. Unfortunately, to his disappointment, he found the throne jealously guarded by a gang of eunuchs who were illiterate and uncivil. However, he managed to extend the Jesuit mission farther north to Nanjing where conversions grew at the rate of a hundred a year. Ricci, even though he did not see the emperor, but so impressed him, that upon Ricci's death he was buried by imperial decree, near the West Wall. To Ricci, however, the Chinese converts were his most significant legacy, not himself. He rejoiced and praised the Lord over the growth of conversions from three in 1584, to about 500 in 1603, and to 2500 in 1610, not big numbers compared to China's population, but he described this as a miracle of God. We may face a different set of problems in our evangelism today, but we should not lose heart.

One of Ricci's legacies was his conversion of Paul Hsu (Xu Guangshi), one of the three pillars of the Chinese Church. Hsu met Ricci in 1600 and asked to be baptized, not only for the impressive scientific learning of the missionaries, but by how far their moral teaching surpassed Confucianism and how much more enlightening their religion was to other religions in China. Hsu's natural ability, intellectual reputation, and integrity of faith and character led him to ever higher appointments in government. He rose to a position, "second only to the emperor." He became the acknowledged leader of the Chinese Christian community.

In this very short account of the early Christian mission, we can learn about our own efforts in reaching out. Pragmatic knowledge or know-how can form the bridge between evangelists and those who do not know God. Our witnessing of the Christian Word and life forms the lasting bond that leads to conversion.

基督教入中國之途徑

基督教與中國最早期的接觸當追溯至7世紀的唐朝；之后是13世紀的元朝。考古學遺留的証據，証實了類似的接觸。

15世紀，葡萄牙人乘船抵達亞洲，在此期間，傳教工作多屬羅馬教會的努力。一位天主教修士方濟各沙勿略(Francis Javior，1506～1552) 曾嘗試借印度與日本為跳板進入中國傳福音，可惜適逢明朝海禁。1552年左右，當他在日本溘然長逝的日子，唯一能做的，僅是眺望遠方的中國海岸。

之後，因為鴉片戰爭，葡萄牙人割據了於廣州之外60英哩的澳門為殖民地，據為己有，作商業發展之用。經過百年發展，澳門成為舉世聞名的東方拉斯維加斯，而當時， 它理所當然地成為對華傳教的門戶，祗是因為明朝的禁海政策，令傳教士難以進入中國。而殖民干擾與文化差異，令傳教事工在澳門變得停滯不前。後來，耶穌會三位極具智慧、才智、與斗志的傳教士：利瑪竇（Matteo Ricci 1552～1610），湯若望（Johann Adam Schall Von Bell 1591～1666），和範禮安（Ferdinand Verbiest1623～1688）的來到，中國的大門被敲開，傳教局面才得以扭轉。

他們駁斥了漢語晦澀難學難學的謬論，推翻了有關中國必須著西式禮服、奉西方禮儀的觀念。這種對不同文化開明包容的思想，成為耶穌會傳教士日後在華傳道的象征。

耶穌會士羅明堅（Michele Ruggieri 1543~1607) 發現，演示西方知識和技術的成果，是吸引中國官方興趣與注意的關鍵。他因送給中國將軍一塊手表引起轟動。籍此，他和利瑪竇被許可在中國停留。

而利瑪竇實在是上帝預備進入中國傳教最理想的人選。此君思想敏銳，記憶極為驚人，且具深厚的數學、天文、與地理方面的建樹。他所展示的世界地圖徹底折服了當時的中國學者，令他們終於了解到，中國並非處於世界的中心。尤需著墨的是，利瑪竇証實了自己極高的語言天份：他不僅能說中文，而且深諳中國古文，並可以書寫數百漢字。他卓越不群，令人難以忘懷，注定是有史以來，中國最為知名的傳教士。

利瑪竇的實踐和經驗令他相信，在華傳教最好的方法，莫過於將所傳的信息達致皇帝的耳中。他的聲譽令一位省長由衷欽佩，於是與他一道，前往北京為皇帝賀壽。但此行卻敗興而歸，因為帝王的寶座竟然被一群不學無術且飛揚跋扈的太監繯繞著。然而，他還是將耶穌會的事工推廣至南京，洗禮人數很快達到一年上百人。

縱然從未與皇帝謀面，但利瑪竇的名字在皇帝心中還是留下了深刻印象。他去世之後，皇帝允准其遺骸葬於北京的平側門（今阜成門）外。對利瑪竇而言，個人算不得什麼，能夠令中國人信主才是最重要的考量和一生最重要的傳奇。無論是最初洗禮的3個人，還是1603年的500人，亦或是1610年的2500人，利瑪竇都將悔改信主的人數歸於上帝的榮耀。雖然這些人數與中國龐大的人口相比極其微不足道，但對於利瑪竇，對於當時的中國，實乃神跡。 今天的福音工作，我們面對的問題或者與利瑪竇的時代極為不同，但我們不當駐足不前。

利瑪竇的另一個傳奇，是他改變了被譽為中國教會三大柱石之一的徐光啟的生命。1660年徐光啟與利瑪竇相遇，徐氏不僅對包括利瑪竇在內的傳教士們豐富的科學知識極為信服，更加受益於其中那些遠勝於孔孟禮教及其他宗教的觀點，遂接受洗禮。後來徐光啟因天資聰穎、博學多聞和誠實穩重而備受賞識，以致他平步青雲，不僅官至禮部尚書，成為皇帝所倚重的朝臣，更成為當時基督教的領袖。

以上對基督教進入中國的簡短介紹，有助於我們反思今天在福音工作外傳中的立場。實用知識是向非基督徒宣教的橋樑。從古至今，傳教事業障礙重重，但若回首利瑪竇的年代，我們就不當灰心氣綏，因為基督之道，與個人生命的見證，必將諦結長遠的關係，達致最後的改變。

Paul of China: Watchman Nee

In the year 1920, a seventeen year old boy named Ni Tuosheng heard the charge by an evangelist, Dora Yu, to believe in Jesus Christ as Lord and Savior. Almost as dramatic as Paul's conversion on the road to Damascus, he accepted the call and consecrated himself to preaching the gospels in China. Just to set the record straight, this was no rash decision by an impressionable youngster in a moment of emotional outburst. Nee was exceptionally bright, a deep thinker, ranking first in all of his classes. His exposure to Christianity was not new. His parents were Christians in Foochow.

At the moment of his salvation, his plans for his promising worldly future were abandoned. He said, "From the evening I was saved, I began to live a new life, for the life of the eternal God had entered into me." He adopted the English name, Watchman, someone chosen by God to sound out a warning call in the dark night. Unlike Paul, he never had formal training in theology. His intelligence, acumen, and discernment enabled him, through diligent studies, to absorb and digest the Bible and the writings of many Christian authors. He was blessed with the tutelage of a mentor, Margaret Barber, a British missionary. Through his early ministry, nearly al his schoolmates were converted and his hometown experienced a revival.

Exhaustion and poverty overtook him and he became seriously ill with tuberculosis and angina pectoris (chest pains). He could have died at any moment, but God granted him his ministry. He said this about his ministry, "When I began to serve the Lord, I was somewhat anxious about the question of my livelihood. Since I was to walk in the Lord's way, I would only rely upon Him to support me. In the year 1921 and 1922, very few preachers in China lived in sole reliance on the Lord. Yet when I looked to the Lord, He said to me, ' If you cannot live by faith, you cannot work for me'. I knew that I needed living work and living faith to serve a living God. God has supplied all my needs and has not failed me once."

He was a firm believer in the oneness of the church and objected to denominational divisions in the church. He championed local churches. From 1923 to 1949, more than 700 local churches were created with attendance more than 70,000. His message spread to south East Asia. His determination in the oneness of the church aroused antagonism among other Christians. Fake rumors and misrepresentations about him and his ministry hurt him. He lamented, "The Watchman Nee portrayed by them I would also condemn."

When the communists came to power in 1949, Nee chose to stay. He asked some of his co-workers to leave China for Taiwan, while he returned to China from the safety of Hong Kong. He told his friend, "What shall we do with so many churches in the Mainland? I must return to take care of them and stand with them for the Lord's testimony." He was following Paul's footsteps (Acts 20:24).

The communists arrested him in 1952 for his belief and his leadership among local churches, and sentenced him to fifteen years of imprisonment. He was not released at the end of the fifteen years. He was never released. The only person who was allowed to visit him was his wife. He died in confinement in 1972, martyr for God. In his final letter, written on the day of his death, he wrote, "In my sickness, I still remain joyful at heart." After he died, a prison guard found a scrap of paper by his bed with these words, "Christ is the Son of God who died for the redemption of sinners and was resurrected after three days. This is the greatest truth in the universe. I die because of my belief in Christ. --Watchman Nee."

教會的守望者: 倪柝聲

1920年，一位名叫倪柝聲的17歲男孩，在Dora Yu的講道中，接受基督為主，他聽聞神的召喚，猶如保羅於大馬色戲劇性的轉化一般，倪柝聲響應這個召喚，奉獻自己於中國傳道。倪柝聲是個出色而優秀之人，自幼受基督信徒雙親影響，對信仰耳熏目染，其轉變絕非一個易受影響的年輕人在突發情緒中，所做的一時衝動的決定。

由決定奉獻傳道的一刻起，他即捨棄了無比美好的前途。他說："由被召喚的那個夜晚，我就有了主所賜的永生。" 倪柝聲為自己起了一個新的英文名字："守望者"：一個被神選擇、於黑夜守望的人。倪柝聲並未受過正式的神學教育，但他憑著其聰穎才智、勤奮學習及敏銳的洞察力來吸收消化聖經和其它基督徒的作品。得益於英國傳教士Margaret Barber的言傳身教，與多數同學一樣，他認識了基督。

無私的奉獻，令倪柝聲集勞成病，弭患肺結核和心絞痛，死亡隨時都會發生。但是主授予他新生，他說："初為主做工時，我為生計憂心。但一踏上為主服務的這條路，基督就成為支持我的力量。1921~1922年的中國，鮮有傳道人靠福音養生，但當我仰望主，因主說:缺乏信心，你便不能為我傳道。自此我曉得，活的上帝需要活的信心去服侍。祂果然供應我一切所需，從未失信。"

倪柝聲深信教會合一，擁護地方教會，反對宗派分歧。由1923年到1949年，他成立了700多家地方教會，超過70，000人參加禮拜，他的信息遠播東南亞。但教會合一的信念卻招致多人的反對，謠言漫天飛，令他及其事工受到很大的傷害。他哀嘆說："反對者口中所描述的倪柝聲，是個連我自己都要譴責的人。"

1949年，共產黨執政，倪柝聲勸告他的同工逃往台灣，而他卻選擇留下。他對朋友說："我們都走了，大陸眾多的教會怎麼辦？我要回去，為了見証的緣故守望教會。" 他追隨的是保羅的腳蹤。(Acts 20:24)

1952年，倪柝聲因其信仰被共產黨以基督徒領袖的名義逮捕，判刑15年。事實上，倪柝聲至死未曾獲釋，反而被隔離起來，他的太太是唯一能到獄中探望之人。 1972年，倪柝聲於监獄殉道。離世之際寫到:"即使患病，我心依然歡欣。" 倪柝聲死後，獄警在其床上發現一張紙片，上面寫到："基督是神的兒子，為救贖罪人而死，三天后復活，此乃宇宙最偉大的真理。我死是因為相信基督。——守望者，倪柝聲。”

Sun Yat Sen and Christian Education

The year of 2011 was the 100th anniversary of the 1911 Revolution in China, overthrowing the Ching Dynasty. There were a number of conferences and celebratory activities commemorating the great event. Professor Peter Tse-ming Ng of the Hong Kong Sheng Kung Hui Episcopal Ming Hua Seminary presented a talk on Dr. Sun Yat Sen's revolution and its connection to Christian influences. It was my great pleasure and honor to be able to contact Professor Ng to learn a few highlights from his talk, which I am sharing with you here. Professor Ng reported that Dr. Sun was greatly influenced and supported by Christian education throughout his life.

As a teenager, Dr. Sun attended Christian schools in Honolulu and Hong Kong even though he was a native of Zhong Shan, China. He was a student at Iolani School of Honolulu and the Diocesan Boys' School in Hong Kong. He was active in church ministries, having absorbed the Christian ideals of truth, sacrifice, service to society, and salvation for the nation and its people. He had great admiration for Washington and Lincoln, and harbored desires to redress the ills of China. The Christian bible accompanied him when he returned from Honolulu to Zhong Shan at the age of seventeen. Soon after, he was baptized in Hong Kong. It was not evangelism alone which touched his heart. It was the total Christian freedom which surrounded him and permeated his mindset. The Christian education he received granted him not only salvation in Christ, but also a committed life for the love of country. He has proved wrong the prevailing saying, "one more Christian, one fewer Chinese."

Dr. Sun chose to study medicine, first at the Canton Hospital (which later became part of Lingnan University) then at the College of Medicine for Chinese in Hong Kong, partly because of the latitude of political ideology. His association with Hong Kong Christians fortified his revolutionary views. He had also built a world-wide network with Christians, in Hong Kong, Southeast Asia, Japan, England, and the United States, who gave him much support for his revolutionary activities. During the revolution, Sun had many followers from the Christian colleges and at one of the events, it was reported that thirty percent of the activists were Christians. One of the leading Christian universities was Lingnan of Canton, which became a stronghold for his insurgency. The spirit of Lingnan was strongly Christian, which showed itself in its inspiring slogans such as, Service, Brotherhood, Freedom, Equality, Patriotism, and Sportsmanship. It is interesting to note that the motto of Lingnan was adapted from that of Yale University, to become: For God, for Country, and for Lingnan. It was estimated that immediately after the revolution in 1912, sixty five percent of the personnel in the provincial government were graduates from Christian colleges. Hence, it cannot be denied that Christianity had brought great change in China since the arrival of the famed missionary, Morrison, two centuries ago, and this was one of the engines behind the 1911 Republican Revolution.

In the annals of Lingnan history, there stood out an inspiring episode. After the success of the 1911 revolution, Kwangtung Province established an initial military government. To support this fledgling government, the Lingnan students organized a fundraising team. With the blessing of the university, the students were allowed a leave of absence from their studies to deploy into three spearheads canvassing Hong Kong, Macao, and Canton. They spent three months to raise $70,000 in silver and a large sack of gold which was a timely contribution to the revolutionary forces. Dr. Sun personally came to Lingnan in 1912 to commend the patriotic students for their exceptional effort. Today's university students can learn much from the heroic acts of Lingnan youths. The president of Lingnan, Dr. Chung Wing Kwong, added his comments, "Everyone knows we are a Christian school. True Christian ideals include sacrificial revolution for the people, applying the knowledge we gained as tools in the service of the masses."

孫中山先生與基督教教育

2011年，是辛亥革命推翻清政府100周年紀念，為此各種紀念活動層出不窮。香港聖公會明華書院的吳梓明教授就孫中山先生發起的辛亥革命運動及其與基督教的淵源發表了講話。本人有幸與吳教授接洽，得以將其談話的要點在此與諸位分享。吳教授述及了基督教教育及業界對孫先生一生的深刻影響及支持。

少年時期，出生於廣東中山的孫先生曾就讀於美國檀香山和香港的拔萃男校。負櫝期間，他活躍於教會事工，汲取了基督教精義中關於真理、無私、服務社會、以及救恩澤國益民的思想。出於對美國總統華盛頓和林肯的欽佩，他的心中燃點著救治苦難中國的理想。當他身攜聖經由美國檀香山返回廣東中山時，年僅17歲。不久，他於香港洗禮。而此時，與其說是宣教的意願撞擊著他，倒不如說對基督教自由理念的追尋令他心潮洶涌。耳熏目染的基督教不僅是救恩的宣揚，更是一種愛國的委身。故此，他要力證當時盛行“多一個基督徒，少一個中國人”的觀念是錯誤的。

基於當時代的政治思想理念，孫先生選擇了醫科，先肆業於廣東醫學院（此院後併入嶺南大學)，後入讀香港的中醫學院。而其革命的觀念，也因與香港基督徒的廣泛接觸而日趨堅定。同期，在香港、東南亞、日本、及英美等地，在基督徒圈子裡，他相継建立了廣博的人脈，這些人曾為他後來的革命事業予以強大的支持。

整個辛亥革命運動中，孫先生身邊大量的追隨者皆來自基督教院校。據稱當時的某個運動裡，有超過三成的參與者是基督徒。廣東的嶺南大學是最為踴躍的追隨者之一，而此校後來成為發動起義的根據地。嶺南大學的精神極具基督教色彩，由其勵志口號可見一斑，如服務、手足情誼、自由、平等、愛國主義、健體強身。令人莞爾的是，嶺南大學的校訓源自美國耶魯大學校訓，奉為：為　上帝、為國家、為嶺南！

曾有人統計過，自辛亥革命後的1912年，有超過六成的政府官員畢業於各基督教院校。由此見證了兩個世紀前，著名宣教士馬禮遜先生將基督教信仰帶入中國的影響是多麼深刻久遠！而對發生於1911年的辛亥革命，基督教更是有著不可忽視的巨大推動力。

讓我們重溫嶺南大學一個鼓舞人心的歷史片段。1911年辛亥革命成功後，廣東省成立了一個雛形的軍人政權。為支援這個初生的新政權，嶺南大學組建了一個為之籌款的團隊， 在學校的鼓勵下，學生可暫停課業，到當時三個興盛的商埠：香港、澳門及廣東展開籌資活動。三個月後，他們將所籌得的七萬兩銀子和大量金子，及時支援了當時的革命運動。

孫先生曾以個人的名義於1912年親臨嶺南，表彰愛國學生的傑出貢獻。嶺南學人的英勇事蹟令現今學子得益良多。嶺南大學校長，鄺博士曾勸勉："作為基督教學校, 嶺南可謂家喻戶曉，但真正的基督教理念當是無私舍己，學以致用，服務人群。"

Early Protestant Missions

Luther posted his famous "Ninety Five Theses" in 1517 which signaled the start of Protestantism. Prior to this date, naturally all missionary work was in the hands of the Catholic Church. Such efforts in China's case dated back to the thirteenth century.

In 1305, the Franciscan John of Montecovino wrote from Peking to Rome. Later, the Catholic monarchs of Europe were required by the Pope to bring the Catholic faith to newly discovered lands.

In view of this backdrop, it was hard to understand the lack of missionary zeal on the part of the reformers. The fact was there was little evidence of concern for overseas missions.

Historians have speculated about the reasons for such inaction. Surprisingly, Luther himself was one of the important obstacles. Even the other leaders of the reformation were unenthusiastic. One possible explanation is that the reformers assumed the Great Commission had been assigned to and fulfilled by the apostles. Myopia was wide spread. Luther said, "No one has any longer such a universal apostolic command, but each bishop or pastor has his appointed diocese or parish." Such indifference could have originated in the insecure and inward looking mentality of the Protestant movement to establish itself during the period of religious wars. Survival in Europe was a much more urgent matter. Adding to this, the Protestant rulers were indifferent to spreading the faith, in contrast to the Papal stimulus for Catholic monarchs. The lack of contact between non- Christian peoples with Protestant countries was another reason. Nationalism following the Reformation focused efforts upon the internal needs of European nations.

It was not until the Westminster Confession of Faith in 1647 that the Great Commission was brought back to center stage, but unsympathetic voices could still be heard. "Through the apostles the Gospels had been conveyed to all and that the Great Commission had been fulfilled and was no longer binding." "If any race or people had failed to respond, it deserved to be judged as heathens. Christian laymen and pastors were not called to be missionaries." Perhaps, the discovery of America and the arrival of the puritans were catalysts in reaching out to the heathens. In the thirteen colonies, as a first experience, Calvinists encountered non-Christian natives in multitudes. In Great Britain, Evangelical Awakening gained strength in the eighteenth century, followed by colonial expansion which brought more exposure to non-Christians. The climax of Protestant missions occurred in the period 1815-1914. The Westminster Confession had an enormous influence. All able-bodied young men and women were urged to be missionaries. There was a surge of missionaries from universities in both Great Britain and America which produced the likes of James Hudson Taylor who was probably the most remembered and loved missionary in China. This article might encourage you to learn from the life in Christ of this Saint.

The Chinese Christian Mission

新教早期的傳教使命

1517年， 馬丁路德發表著名的《95條論綱》，標誌著新教的開始。此前所有的傳教工作，自然是掌握在羅馬天主教的手中，他們在中國的努力則可追溯到十三世紀。1305年，方濟各會的孟高維諾由北京寫信至羅馬，導致後來教皇要求歐洲各國君主，將天主教的信仰帶到新發現的領地去。

在如此背景下，令人費解的是，改教者的宣教熱忱卻不甚高漲。這一點由今日甚難找到當時海外宣教的資料可見一斑。

史學家們曾多方揣測如此不作為的原因。認為除了領導者缺乏改革熱情，路德本人是一個重要的障礙。另一種解釋是，改革者認為"大使命"已經被使徒們實現了，甚至路德本人都說，"再沒有什麼使徒命令了，祇是主教與牧師各有自己指定的教區或堂區"， 視野極為狹窄。相對教皇對下屬傳教的要求，新教領導層對傳播信仰則無動於衷，此種漠不關心大約始於宗教戰爭期間，新教初始之時。他們認為燃眉之急是如何在歐洲站穩腳跟，為確立自己的地位而出現的浮躁與固守顯而易見。

傳教冷漠的另一個原因，是新教與非基督教國家之間缺乏溝通與接觸。改革者民族至上的精神，使宣教重點被置與歐洲大地內在的需求上。

直到1647年，威斯敏斯特信條發布，大使命才得以重新被重視，但反對的聲音仍然不絕於耳："籍著使徒，福音已經傳遍天下，大使命經已完成"。"凡忽略、或不作回應的種族，當受永恆的懲罰。基督教平信徒和牧師不是被召作傳教士的"。

或者，要等到清教徒登上美洲大陸，傳教的熱忱和意念才被激發出來。在十三個殖民地，加爾文主義者首次遭遇了大量非基督教的土人。而在英國，伴隨著 殖民擴張，18世紀的大覺醒運動增強了傳教的力度。新教徒宣教的高潮更於1815年至1914年期間被推至巔峰。其中威斯敏斯特信條產生著巨大的影響。許多體格健壯的男男女女都渴望參與到宣教當中。英國和美國的大學裡，涌現了大量如戴德生一般既令人難忘又倍受中國人傳頌的傳教士。

撰寫此文，是希望我們能有機會學習並效法宣教聖徒們在基督裡的生命。

Himalayas to Our Town

In 1908, an English young man, James Outran Fraser, dedicated his life to missionary work in the remote province of China, Yunnan, in the Himalayan foothills of the Burma-Tibet mountains where the Lisu minority lived. Books have been written about his passion for the gospels. I should like to extract from his vast and valuable experience and keen observations an apt vignette which can serve our own ministries today here in our city with wisdom of the ages. You might think that there are few parallels between the missions of such disparate geographies and times. A very relevant connection between the mission of this saint and ours is the cultural gap that existed then and which exists now. These cultural divergences obstruct evangelistic work in major ways. In the early 20th century, most Chinese have not heard the gospel message at all. Probably fewer than one in a hundred had any intelligent knowledge of Christianity. When they came into contact, they invariably conceived the message to mean for people to do good and nothing more. Christianity was just being raised to the level of most pagan religions from that of an irrelevant foreign fairy tale. This sadly is still the situation today among the non-believers in our community. It is a foreign religion, then and now. Every race or country has its own religion. Christianity was an English religion to the Chinese. Now, maybe Anglo-American, or perhaps Roman. The Chinese in general were and are not deep religious thinkers from a philosophical point of view. After thousands of years, they have, as a race, failed to evolve one consistent religious system and develop it deeply. Their religions are more external than internal. Forms exist because ancestors did so. "You have your way and we have ours, so why argue?" It is a remarkable fact that this intelligent race, after 4000 years of history, has gone so far astray from the universal truth as practically to forget the very existence of the One True God, the creator. We are not addressing the atheism of communism but rather the endemic Chinese mentality of the ages.

Temporal benefits outweigh all other considerations, just as with other Chinese religions. The gospels are looked at in the light of a business proposition. They want to know if becoming a Christian will ward off calamities, or enable one to gain riches as pagan worship is supposed to. We are faced with the same barriers. Do we not see the statues of local gods in many shops, with candles or incense before them and fruit offerings? We need every member's input on how we may reach out and touch our neighbors. We have the cultural exposure, more than others. They have not cried for us to "come" but the Lord has commanded us to "go".

從喜馬拉雅到我們的城市

1908年，一位名叫James Outram Fraser 的年輕人，立志將生命奉獻給中國雲南坐落於喜馬拉雅山腳傈僳族人居住的地方。雖然有很多關於他福音使命的著述，我仍希望將他廣泛珍貴的經驗及其銳利的觀察採集如下，為我們今天的事工提供參考。你或者以為地域不同、時代不同，其中未必有可取之處。但無論當年的聖工，還是今天的服侍，雙方都要面對文化的代溝。文化代溝隨處可見。

20世紀初，多數中國人尚未聽過福音， 更遑論受過教育的基督徒。所傳的福音信息除了被一成不變地注解為做善事外，別無他物。基督教成為與其他社群無異的宗教，可惜類似狀況至今依然存在。至於共產主義，在傳統中國文化中，則屬地方性心理。

無論過去還是現在，對中國人來說，基督教祇是一個外國宗教。每個族類和國家都有其獨特的宗教，基督教則是進到中國的英美宗教，或羅馬宗教。中國人一向不是深刻的宗教思想家，幾千年來，作為一個民族，他們從未發展出一個貫徹如一、屬於自己、並嘗試遵循與恪守的宗教體系。中國宗教注重外在形式，與古人亦步亦趨，各有套路，不必爭拗。我要討論的，非共產主義無神論，乃一個值得留意的事實：中國，如此智慧充滿的族類，長達4000余年歷史，卻一直遠離獨一真神，且迷失得如此遙遠。眼前的利益與好處對人們來說價值更高、更實在。福音被淪為生意的命題，是否選擇信教的首要考慮是，此教能否幫我避凶就吉----實與異教無異。

今天教會面對的是同樣的障礙，我們需要思考如何跨越這些障礙，去接觸相近的鄰舍。今天，文化方面的障礙相對更多。人們或許不會說："你來吧！"，但主耶穌的命令則是"你們去！"

Chung Wing Kwong: A Christian Educator

Chung Wing Kwong was born in 1866 during the era of China's notorious weakness. The Manchu (Qing) dynasty was in decline, both physically and morally. The Sick Man of Asia was under siege internally and externally. Illiteracy was widespread, along with slavery, concubinage, foot binding, and opium smoking.

Chung was a brilliant student with a photographic memory who distinguished himself in national examinations. Sadly, the current of the times swept him into a dissolute life of cynicism. He even worked as a "ghost writer" sitting in examinations for candidates who paid for this service.

Later in the nineteenth century, the Presbyterian Foreign Mission of the U. S. sent missionaries to southern China to spread the Gospel through medical and educational work. Rev. Dr. A. P. Happer and Rev. B. C. Henry were the vanguards in the effort to raise educated men to be Christian ministers, teachers, and physicians, as well as for every other calling in life, by teaching western science, medicine, and religion, in English. It was through this light that Chung decided he needed a change in direction in his life. He became a follower of Christ. As an established and matured scholar of Chinese culture, he was admitted to study at the Canton Christian College, as a beginning student of English. In 1905, Chung graduated from the middle-school preparatory class. He was already thirty nine years old. He was both a teacher of Chinese and a student of English at the school. His reputation as a scholar attracted students for the school, as a bridge between cultures of East and West. In 1926, the college became Lingnan University and Chung was chosen for its presidency in 1927.

Throughout his life, Chung did not seek fame or profit. He devoted himself to prayer and reading the bible. He delivered sermons in various churches and schools. We may learn from his confidence in doing God's work from an interview about his notable fundraising accomplishments.

Reporter: "Teacher, your fundraising manner has become well-known. But I would like to know, how do you find so much courage when you are asking strangers for money?"

Chung: "My fundraising is for a righteous cause, so it is not I who asks; rather it is the donor who asks me to accept. I have given face to people; if they choose not to give face to me, then it does not affect my position. Therefore, others should feel ashamed, not I."

Chung was saying that when our cause is righteous, we should take courage. Those not responding to righteousness should be the ones who feel ashamed.

A Lingnan alumnus, Professor Lee Shao-cheung of Hawaii recalls a private "sermon" from Chung: "Jesus Christ was a perfect man. He was able to accomplish what the sages and earlier generations could not. He washed out all of our sins and was reborn in a victorious life...." When Chung asked Lee to kneel down and pray, Lee was moved to tears. He remained grateful to this day.

Regardless of our background or gifts, God calls each of us to work for His glory, empowering us in discipleship. Let learn from Chung Wing Kwong to spread God's word in his own way, even as laymen.

基督教教育家：鐘永光

鐘永光1866年出生，時值中國最丑陋、軟弱的年代。清政府日趨衰落、國家道德滑坡、破爛不堪；人民貧窮，文盲俯首皆是，東亞病夫內憂外患。此外，奴隸、蓄婢、扎腳、鴉片......

當時的鐘永光是個出色的學生，俱過目不忘之本領，在國家狀元科舉考試中出類拔萃。可惜受時代熏染，曾經過著憤世嫉俗的放蕩生活。為了錢的缘故，他甚至代他人赴考。

19世紀末，美國長老會對外宣教機構差派一批傳教士前往南中國，以醫學和教育為渠道向中國人傳福音，並幫助培育基督教的牧師、教師和醫生，其范圍涵括了各種專業性的職業。這些傳教士以英文教授西方的科學、醫學、宗教。

在此境況中，鐘永光決定信耶穌，改變生活的方向。作為一位頗有建樹與成就的中國學人，他被廣州基督教學堂錄取，修讀英文。1905年，當鐘永光於大學預科學堂畢業的時候，已年屆39歲。在校讀書的日子，他既是中文教師又是英文學生。其學者的榮譽，曾影響和吸引著大批學生前來就讀，如同一座橋梁，他將東西雙方締結為一。

1926年，此學堂更名為嶺南大學；1927年，鐘永光榮任首位華人校長。終其一生，他不計名譽財富，卻委身禱告讀經，並於不同的教會與學校講道。籌款有成的他，與記者的對答，令我們看見他對聖工的自信。記者問他說，“校長，你籌款的方法街知巷聞，你是如何得著向陌生人籌款的勇氣呢？”鐘永光說，“我籌款是為了正義事業，因此不是我乞求人，乃是人來求我去接受他們的捐款，是我給他們面子。倘若他們不賞面，我絕不會感到難為情，拒絕捐款的人才真的感到難為情。”是的，如果我們的事業是公義的，就當有勇氣，對公義事業缺乏回應之人，才當羞愧。

一位夏威夷的嶺南校友名李紹祥，對舊時鐘永光的一份私人講章記憶猶新，鐘永光說：“耶穌是個完人，祂所成就的，令歷世之人望其項背；祂洗去人的罪，重生於得勝的生命......”。鐘永光曾邀請李紹祥跪下禱告，李感動的泣然淚下，至今記憶猶新。無論背景天賦如何，上帝呼召我們、賦予門徒的權柄，為祂的榮耀做工，讓我們學效鐘永光，雖非牧者，卻能傳揚基督，彰顯祂公義，榮耀的名。

China's Hudson Taylor

Hudson Taylor did not know that his father prayed to God for his son to become a missionary to China. The young Hudson was not cooperating until his mother prayed in solitude for his conversion when he was seventeen. He heard the call. They simultaneously broke the good news to each other, like announcing a miracle.

Hudson had the gift of languages and studied Greek, Hebrew, Latin, and Mandarin on his own. He tested his missionary spirit by ministering to the poor in Yorkshire, England. God proved to him that He would be faithful and would provide for his needs, a trust which Hudson never forgot. Before he completed his medical training in London, he set sail for China in a perilous voyage in 1854. Once in China, his physical and mental constitutions were tested to the limit. He teamed up with the English Presbyterian Mission at first. In Swatow, the tropical summer and the stench of night soil made him very sick.

On top of this, his medical supplies for his ministry were destroyed by fire. He was also robbed of all his possessions including his Bible. The mission was also out of funds. Many people, including other missionaries ridiculed him for adopting the Chinese way of dress and living, a hint of the future "pigtail mission." He became an independent missionary funded only by faith. God blessed him with a missionary wife, Maria Dyer who sustained his work. During his furlough in England for health reasons, he prayed for 24 volunteers to go back to China with him. His prayer was answered and much money was raised.

The mission was set up in Hangzhow. Some of the Taylor children died in China. It was a xenophobic time in China and the mission was persecuted. His heroic wife died and the surviving children had to be sent back to England. Health problems continued to plague him but God was faithful and answered his prayers for more missionary workers and more money support.

By 1885, his mission consisted of 225 missionaries, 59 churches and 1655 members.

In 1887, he prayed for another 100 new workers. In fact, 600 answered the call, but he could only accept 102. He prayed for $50,000 but raised $105,000. He even acquired 14 volunteers from America. His work included a translation of the New Testament.

In 1900, Hudson was semi-retired in Europe due to ill health. News of the Boxer Rebellion and the resulting riots and massacres of Christian devastated him. He gasped, "I cannot read, I cannot pray, I can scarcely think….but I can trust ! "

In 1905, the frail Hudson returned to China. He died on this trip and was buried near his wife, Maria, in Chinking. He had spent 51 years in and out of China, establishing the famous China Inland Mission. He brought 849 missionaries to the field, trained some 700 Chinese workers, raised 4 million dollars, and developed a Chinese church of 125,000.

Because of Hudson, China became a household word among English speaking countries. He is well remembered and loved.

One of his quotes: "Christ is either Lord of all, or is not Lord at all."

中國的戴德生

戴德生並不知道他的父親曾祈禱上帝，讓他到中國成為一個傳教士。年輕的戴德生並不情願，直到17歲母親獨自為他的生命改變而祈禱。如同一個奇蹟，他生命改變、回應呼召，與母親的禱告蒙應允幾乎同時發生。

戴德生具語言的天賦，自修希臘文，希伯來文，拉丁文和普通話。在英國的約克郡，他透過服侍窮人，來測試自己的勇氣。上帝向他證明祂的信實，並應允提供他一切需求。完成倫敦的醫療訓練之前，於1854一次危險的航程中前往中國。抵達後，他的身體、精神諸方面的能力受到極限的考驗。在汕頭，熱帶的夏季和糞便的惡臭讓他感到噁心。最初的日子，他與英國長老會彼此聯手。

至為可惜的是，為事工預備的醫療用品被大火燒毀，所有的財產，包括他的《聖經》被搶劫，傳教缺乏經費。許多人，包括傳教士，都在嘲笑他的中國服飾與生活，令他成為唯一靠信仰過活的獨立傳教士。神賜福給他一個傳教士的妻子，瑪麗亞·代爾支持他的工作。後來， 他因健康原因回英國休假期間，他曾祈禱24名志願者與他一同回中國服侍，其禱告不但得蒙允准，此次休假還籌集到較多的傳教經費。

傳教事工成立於杭州。當時，中國適逢排外時期，傳教事工遭受迫害。戴德生英勇的妻子去世，孩子有的死於中國，倖存的則被送返英國。健康問題繼續困擾著他，但上帝信實地答應他的祈禱，他有了更多的傳教同工及更多的資金支持。

1885年，戴德生的事工包括225個傳教士，59個教會和1655名成員。

1887年，他祈禱另外100名新同工，得到的是600人的回應，他祗能接受102位。他為五萬美元祈禱，得到的是十萬零五千美元，還獲得來自美國14名志願者的支持。當時戴德生的工作包括新約翻譯。

1900年，由於健康欠佳，戴德生在歐洲半退休。義和團運動的新聞，暴亂和屠殺基督徒的消息令他傷心欲絕。他氣喘吁吁地說，“我不能阅讀，我不能祈禱，我不能想象......但我仍然相信！”

1905年，體弱多病的戴德生重返中國， 卻死於旅途，於重慶與愛妻瑪麗亞同葬。當中51年，他出入中國並建立了著名的中國內地會。他帶領849名傳教士加入宣教工廠，培訓了約700名中國同工，籌集了400萬美元，建立了約125,000人的教會。

由於戴德生，許多的英語國家裡，中國，成為一個家喻戶曉的名字。而他則倍受懷念和愛戴。他其中一句格言，“基督若不是萬有的主，祂就不是主。”

Robert Morrison in 19th Century China

"What then do the Chinese require from Europe? Not the arts of reading and printing; not merely general education; not...... civilization; they require that only which St. Paul deemed supremely excellent, and which it is the sole object of the Missionary Society to communicate--they require the knowledge of Christ." Robert Morrison (1824).

It may be surprising to most people that Nestorian Christianity had reached China in the 7th century AD during the Tang Dynasty. The Roman Catholics came in the 13th century. Each wave of Christian appearance faded with the fortunes of the respective Chinese regime. Again, near 1600 AD, the Jesuits made great progress, having the ears of emperors with their science and especially astronomy. Sadly, they eventually faced persecution as different Christian missions attacked each other's approach in dealing with local religions. The gathering European imperialism also aroused antipathy. Christianity was actually banned in 1800. One observer remarked, "The wonder is, not that Christianity was persecuted, but that it was allowed to exist at all." So, how then did a Presbyterian Scot, Robert Morrison, cast the seeds of Protestantism in China in the early 19th century? The answer predictably is, with much difficulty and sacrifice.

Born in 1782 to devout parents, the teenage Robert fell into dissolute life which only gave him a burden of sin. He repented. Thereafter, the Bible or some Christian book was always open before him for years to come. He was a brilliant scholar, learning Latin, Greek, Hebrew, theology, and shorthand at the same time beginning in 1801.

He was ordained in January 1807, but before that, he prepared himself for missionary work by studying medicine, astronomy, and Chinese, in London. He knew that the only foreigners permitted on Chinese soil were traders, but he could not forget the 350 million souls without the gospels. His famous prayer was: that God would station him in that part of the missionary field where the difficulties were greatest and all too human appearances the most insurmountable. God answered his prayer pointedly by letting him go to China. He soon faced the difficulties he so desired.

The Chinese were forbidden to teach their language to any foreigner under the penalty of death. No one could remain in China except for trade. The Roman Catholics in Macau under Portuguese protection were hostile towards any Protestant missionary. He had to pretend to be a less hated American trader. His secret tuition in Chinese was most perilous.

His life was utter loneliness. The Chinese cheated him mercilessly. He even tried to conform by adopting the Chinese diet and wearing Chinese garments. Still, he failed to make progress. He was a fugitive missionary hiding his true purpose as well as the Chinese books from which he tried to learn the language. However, he remembered his own reply to the question, "Mr. Morrison, you really expect that you will make an impression on the idolatry of the great Chinese Empire?" His reply was, "No, Sir, I expect God will." In the back of his mind, he realized the importance of learning the language in order to preach, to produce a dictionary, and to translate the bible for the future missionaries.

His health deteriorated under such arduous conditions. What saved him was employment by the East India Company who saw value in his knowledge of the language. He married but his wife died not long after giving birth to three children. He labored to produce a Chinese grammar, a dictionary, and to translate the bible under the threat of death penalty. To his dying day, China did not open up for Christian evangelism. He had to move his work off shore to the Malay Peninsula where he could educate the Chinese there outside of China's law. The educational and printing work went well in Malacca, to help with the spread of the gospels in Asia, and even back into China.

It is quite understandable that Morrison put his efforts into the first complete translation of the bible into Chinese in 1819 in cooperation with another saint, William Milne, the Chinese grammar, and the Chinese-English dictionary. Subsequent generations of missionaries benefited immensely from these pioneering works. Robert Morrison is considered by many as the most influential China missionary.

He died in Canton in 1834. His name is memorialized prominently in Hong Kong.

十九世紀馬禮遜牧師在中國

馬禮遜先生曾於1824年說過：中國人能夠從歐洲得著什麼助益呢？既非藝術的創作，亦非文化的教育，更不是文明的鑄造；中國人所需要的恰是使徒保羅所說、也是眾傳教團體所致力的主題----對基督的認識！

歷史上鮮為人知的是，公元七世紀之前，基督教即已傳入中國唐朝，而到了公元十三世紀，羅馬天主教才進入中國。歷史的更迭中，基督教在中國的每一次潮湧似乎都留痕甚微。直至近十五世紀，耶穌會才取得了顯著的成效，并引起當時皇帝對其所帶入的科學、尤其是天文學的興趣。無奈，他們卻受到當地宗教的攻擊，與數世紀前的先驅們如出一轍，而歐洲諸國對中國的攫取亦引致國人無比的反感。事實上，十八世紀，基督教在中國是處於被取締的狀態的。但報導則說："令人驚嘆的是，基督教並未受到迫害，一切都可以自由進行。"這是英國長老會馬禮遜牧師，於十九世紀早葉，將福音的種子撒入中國大地的佐証嗎？答案是：他為此曾付諸了極為沉重的代價。

1782年，馬禮遜出生於一個虔誠的基督教家庭；少年時期的馬禮遜曾沉淪於令其徒生罪咎的世俗生活。悔改後，他沉醉於聖經及聖徒書籍。1801年，他開始研習拉丁文、希臘文、希伯來文、神學及基礎速記，最終成為一位學富五車的泰斗。

1807年他接受按立，被授予牧職。但在此之前，他已於倫敦就未來的宣教事業，於醫學、天文學和中文等方面進行了刻意的裝備。他很清楚當時的外國人衹能以商人的身份進入中國，他心系三億五千萬未聞福音的靈魂，在他那段聞名於世的禱告裡，他曾這樣說：求神會將他放置於一個看似最不可能，且人皆冥頑不靈的環境裡。而 神垂聽了他的禱告，將他帶入中國。他迅即投身於曾經期盼的艱苦當中。

當時的清政府採取閉關自守的政策，嚴禁將漢語教授給任何外國人，違者將處於極刑。除了商貿活動外，沒有任何外國人可以滯留中國。而受庇於葡萄牙政府，活躍於澳門的天主教則非常敵視任何的基督教宣教活動。所以，馬禮遜牧師衹能裝扮成在中國待遇稍好一點的美國商人，而他隱密進行的中文學習則危機重重。

他的生活孤苦無援，當地華人殘忍地欺詐他，為緩解敵對的情緒，他改食中餐，穿戴華人服飾。即便如此，他仍舊舉步維艱。這個亡命的傳教士不得不將中文書籍及自己的宣教意圖統統隱藏起來。然而，他清楚地記得，他對那些曾質疑他的人的回應："馬禮遜先生，你確信你能夠為中國偶像崇拜的陋習帶去改變嗎？"他回答說："不，先生，我祇相信　神能夠。"內心深處，他很清醒掌握當地語言對佈道事工、對發行字典、為未來的傳教士翻譯聖經是多麼重要。

在惡劣的環境下，他的健康每況愈下，此時，看重其語言才華的東印度公司雇佣了他，並提供了及時的協助。他進入婚姻，但其妻在生育了三個孩子後不久即撒手人寰。在如此艱難的處境中，他仍不斷地致力於漢語文法，『華英辭典』的編纂以及翻譯聖經。在其生命的尾聲，清廷仍未對基督教宣教打開國門，他不得不將未竟的事業轉移到馬來半島的馬六甲，以至於他可以在大清律法管轄之外栽培中國人。馬六甲的教育與印刷的事業發展順利，不但促進了福音在亞洲的傳播，甚至進而回到中國。

1819年，馬禮遜牧師完成中國歷史上首版基督教（新教）中文聖經的翻譯。隨後他與另外一位宣教聖徒米憐牧師攜手，令中文文法和『華英詞典』相繼出版，從而後人可從一個更為開闊的眼界解讀傳教士被拒於清廷國門之外的這段歷史。這些拓荒先驅的工作令後來世代的宣教事業受益無窮，而馬禮遜牧師可謂眾多宣教先驅中最具影響力的一位。

1834年馬禮遜牧師歿於廣東，他的名字被銘刻於世人心中，其工作的果效無遠佛居。

An English Missionary, William Milne, and the first Hakka Chinese Evangelist, Liang Fa

Rev. Robert Morrison crossed many oceans as the lone Protestant missionary to China in 1807 and to struggle for seven years before any help would come: One was a preacher from England, three years his junior, William Milne. Another was Milne's spiritual son, Liang Fa, a Hakka (a minority people in China with a distinct language, literally guest people) Chinese youngster who later was ordained by Morrison as the first recorded Chinese Christian evangelist.

Morrison was under the protection of the chartered traders as a translator, but Milne did not come under the same protection of the East India Company and for that reason was not permitted to evangelize in China, even surreptitiously. He had to work in Malacca, looking longingly into China.

Milne was a most brilliant and capable scholar and an outstanding evangelist. He made the famous grudging observation concerning the Chinese language: "To acquire the Chinese language is a work for men with bodies of brass, lungs of steel, heads of oak....eyes of eagles, hearts of apostles, memories of angels, and lives of Methuselah!" He cooperated with Morrison to translate the entire bible. He was instrumental in organizing the Christian publishing efforts in Malacca. Christian literature became widely available because of him. He and Morrison founded the famous Anglo-Chinese College in Malacca, to train Chinese evangelists for China from the safety of a British colony. His Chinese spiritual paper, Two Friends, became the most widely read single piece of Christian literature in China in the nineteenth and into the twentieth century. The opium trade was repugnant to him, which he called the "curse of China."

His life was beset with unbearable sorrow and hardship. His young wife died in China leaving him with four children. His own health was also weakened beyond repair. Despite such challenges, he managed to publish the first Chinese language magazine. His Chinese-Anglo College was later transplanted to Hong Kong, as Ying Wa College. Unwittingly, he performed one of the most memorable acts of his short but inspiring ministry with lasting effects. He baptized Liang Fa, his printing aide who read all of Milne's prodigious writing. Milne never pressured him but prayed for his fellow worker and loyal friend. When Liang Fa decided to receive baptism into Christ, Milne wrote, "He was no longer a servant, but more than a servant, a brother beloved."

Liang became the first Chinese evangelist. Being a learned person in Chinese literature, Liang easily combined the Chinese mentality with the

Christian doctrines as he read and heard them from Morrison and Milne. His printing and publishing skills made him an indispensable worker in God's service. One of his quotes is long remembered: "It is desirable that the men of this great and glorious Middle Kingdom... should not boast vainly of their own country's being the land of propriety and righteousness as well as of fine literature. They should humbly cast aside their prejudices regarding the country in which Christianity originated and instead consider that the God of Heaven created us as human beings. Everyone who is human ought to know the saving doctrines of the bible." (1832)

Milne, in his short missionary life (he died at 37 unlike Methuselah), accomplished much more than those who lived to old age. The fruits of his work have stayed with us today even if not many of us remember his name.

英国傳教士米憐與中国客家傳道人梁發

1807年,馬禮遜牧師孤身一人遠涉重洋，因基督的愛來到中華這片福音未墾之原，於無援無助的情形下默默工作了七年，直到一位年幼於他三歲的英國牧師威廉.米憐的到來。其後的同工則是米憐牧師所結的果子—梁發，一位年輕的廣東客家人，被馬禮遜按立為牧師的第一位中國人。

與馬禮遜不同的是，米憐並沒有東印度公司中的庇護，故不得於中國傳教，即便是隱密地進行亦不可。他不得不暫居馬六甲遙望中華大地。

米憐是一位滿有恩賜兼實幹型的博學之士及傑出的佈道家。對中文學習有異常獨到的見解："若要想學好中文，必須具有銅的軀體、鐵的肺腑、橡樹的頭、彈簧的手、鷹的眼睛、使徒的心、天使般的記憶和瑪土撒拉的壽數"。他與馬禮遜齊心協力完成了整本的聖經翻譯。他幫助完善了馬六甲的基督教出版事業，令當時的基督教刊物唾手可得。他與馬禮遜牧師攜手創辦著名的馬六甲英華書院，旨在為中國輸送華人宣教士。他的中文講道集《兩個朋友》，乃十九及二十世紀初中國廣泛傳播的基督教刊物。他是鴉片貿易堅定的抵制者，稱鴉片為"中國的咒詛"。

米憐平生可用"歷盡滄桑" 盡訴。年輕的妻子在中國病逝，留下四個年幼的孩子；而他本人的身體狀況亦日趨惡化。面對諸般挑戰，他堅持出版了第一份中文報刊《察世俗每月統紀傳》。所創立的英華書院隨後遷至香港，定名英華學院。米憐在其短暫卻輝煌的一生中所取得的成就對後世有著無法估量的影響。由他施洗的梁發，作為其所聘用的印刷工人對他多產的著作受益無盡。米憐從不強迫他人，素以禱告守望來紀念他的同事及朋友。當梁發要求並接受洗禮時，米憐曾寫到："他不再是僕人，他甚於僕人，乃被愛之弟兄。"

梁發是首位華人佈道家，曾受教於中國舊私塾，較易將基督教義融入國人思維。而他印刷及出版的技能，則有助他堅持不懈於宣教事工。他曾經說過："我期盼生長於廣博富饒的中華大地的人們，不可妄自誇耀為禮義之邦。當謙卑地放下其對以基督教義立國之邦的偏見，進而思想上天之 神造人的旨意何在。人之為人就當清楚聖經言及的救贖之道。"（1832）

在米憐短暫的宣教生涯中（他僅在世37年），其成就遠遠超過許多高壽之人。其名字或許不為人知，但其影響至今猶存。

Rev. Dr. Andrew P. Happer, Founder of the First Presbyterian Church in Canton

The name, Lingnan, to most first generation Chinese immigrants invariably commanded respect and warmth, born of learning and the fond memory of Chinese-American friendship. Lingnan became an influential university for south China, pioneered by the American Presbyterian Church. The epic story of Lingnan's rise from a Boys' School to a Christian College and finally to a university with a strong Christian spirit, will be the subject of another narrative. The tale at hand focuses on its very beginning, still a dream for a dogged missionary, Rev. Dr. Andrew P. Happer who founded the First Presbyterian Church in Canton in 1862.

Dr. Happer was a well-educated man, a graduate of Jefferson College and Western Theological Seminary, and then of the Medical School of the University of Pennsylvania. He arrived China in 1844, after a four month voyage and stayed for forty seven years. At one time, he was the only Presbyterian in south China, to establish the Canton Mission of the American Presbyterian Church. The measure of the man is not his fame but how he met his challenges which were formidable and many. He faced serious health problems while three consecutive wives died during his stay in China. More than once, his life was thought to be spent, but he survived with renewed energy. At the start of his missionary work, the Christian message met with indifference or hostility but he soon learned to use his medical skills to win friends and eventually the tide turned and may people in the Canton area became Christians. Despite this success, he turned his clinic over to his colleague, Dr. John G. Kerr, who later became a legend in medical missionary work. This move was based on Dr. Happer's idea of education alongside evangelism. He could see that the Chinese system of education restricting itself to the books of Confucius produced no correct knowledge of the natural sciences, medicine, and religion. He sensed that English would be an indispensable medium. His insight was prophetic: With Mandarin and English, the graduates from his college will be citizens of the world. Dr. happer was paid $800 a year, equal to $3200 in 1963 dollars and that sum was for both him and his wife, two people teaching for one salary. Such was the dedication of this missionary.

By 1864, he had established schools to train preachers and teachers. After mastering the Chinese language and gaining experience training workers for his mission, a college began in 1888 with 30 students. Dr. and Mrs. Happer constituted two out of the three teaching staff. The third member was a Honolulu Chinese returnee who taught Chinese classics while the Happers taught English. The schedule was 6 hours a day, 6 days a week. Each day began with morning prayer. On Sunday, Bible classes were conducted for four hours. Prayer meetings were held on Sunday and Wednesday evenings. The goal of the school was to prepare Chinese students in English so they will be able to receive instructions through this medium in other subjects later. The intensity of teaching took its toll. Both Happers fell ill in the third year and the school was reluctantly closed in 1890, but Dr. Happer did not give up his dream. He returned to America to rally support for an expanded college. He had a larger vision, to provide western education for the future leaders of China. He sympathizes with the Chinese people, opposing the U.S. Chinese Exclusion Acts. Sadly, he never saw the blossoming of his college into the Lingnan University.

History has not been fair to Dr. Happer. He toiled against all odds and accomplished much despite poor health and heavy family burdens. His uncompromising character and single-mindedness often handicapped him. Paul said: I have fought the good fight. I have finished the race. I have kept the faith. Dr. Happer ran the good race, fought the good fight, and kept the faith.

May Paul's words and the legacy of Dr. Happer inspire us to step forward when God calls.

廣州首位長老教會的發起人哈巴安德牧師

每逢提起"嶺南"二字，老華僑尊敬與愛戴之情都會油然而生。它既是教育的發源地，又是中美友好的象徵。嶺南大學由美國基督教長老會創立，前身是一間男子學校，後發展為基督教學院，最後成為以基督教義為根基的中國著名學府。關於這一點，將另撰文贅述，而所有這些成果，最初祇是傳教士哈巴安德牧師（Dr. Andrew P. Happer）頑強的夢想。

哈巴安德牧師是一名受過高等教育的博士。於Jefferson College和Western Theological Seminary畢業後，他前往賓夕法尼亞州立大學（University of Pennsylvania）並獲得醫學博士學位；其後，歷時4個月的海上顛簸，哈巴安德牧師於1844年抵達中國，并在此服侍達47年之久。曾幾何時，他是當時長老宗在南中國唯一的會員，肩負著長老會在廣州開設教會的重擔。

衡量一個人的偉大，不是基於他的名氣，而是他如何面對無數次強大的挑戰。哈巴安德牧師曾經歷許多病痛，而其妻與兩位續弦亦先後於中國離世。曾幾何時，他似乎命已該絕，但靠著更新的力量，他總得以保存。1862年，隨著第一間長老會在廣州創辦，哈巴安德牧師揭開了這個偉大故事的首卷。

初傳福音的時侯，人們反應冷淡，甚至厭惡。很快，他發現巧用醫術可以贏得朋友，從此頹廢情勢得以扭轉，許多人因此聽聞福音。在此成就下，他再接再勵，將診所改成醫學院；其後，因其以教育輔助福音事工的理念，及約翰-克爾醫生----另一位傳奇傳教士的加入，一個號稱醫學宣教的偉大運動就此展開。

他看到，中國傳統教育的弊端是孔孟道學至上，而忽略自然科學、醫學和宗教。因而他頓悟，英文將是未來世界不可或缺的媒介。而他的洞察力是極具預見性的：唯有掌握好國語與英文，學院的畢業生才會所向無敵，有機會成為這個世界的公民。1963年哈巴安德牧師夫婦一年年薪合起來僅有800元，相當於今天的3200美元，實乃救人靈魂奉獻一切極美的見証。

1864年，哈巴安德牧師再次創立學校，用以培訓傳教士和老師。在掌握了中文，積累了培訓的經驗之後，1888年他創建了一間有著30個學生的學校，目標是透過教授英語使中國學生了解世界。當時在職教師僅有3名：哈巴安德牧師夫婦教授英文，一位從夏威夷歸國的華僑則教授中文。

他們的課時表是一周6天、每天上課6小時，以晨禱開始一天的學習。禮拜天則有4小時的聖經課。而逢周三與主日晚上還有祈禱會。哈巴安德牧師辦學的目標是讓中國學生掌握英文這門語言，將來可以得到更多的機會，明確的教學宗旨令其辦學的目標得以實現。

長期超負荷的工作，令哈巴安德牧師夫婦積勞成疾，在任教的第三年就病倒了，學校不得不於1890年關閉。雖然如此，哈巴安德牧師並未放棄他的夢想。他回到美國，繼續為他擴大在中國的教育四處籌款。此時的他，內心有著一個更美的遠像，就是為中國未來的領袖提供西方的教育。他體恤中國人民，反對美國的排華法案。遺憾的是，在其生前，他並沒有看到自己所創辦的學校發展成為後來的嶺南大學。

歷史對哈巴安德牧師是嚴苛的。他曾歷盡惡劣的健康問題及連番不斷的喪妻之痛，甚至多次死裡逃生，但他不屈不撓地克服所有的艱難，貢獻生命。縱然承受無數的非人之苦，事工倍受羈絆，甚至歷史也不曾公正地對待他，但是他的生命就像保羅說過的話：那美好的仗我已經打過了，當跑的路我已經跑盡了，所信的道我已經守住了……

的確如此，哈巴安德牧師為福音的緣故，跑路、打仗、守道，而上帝為他存留的，將是天上那永不衰殘的榮耀冠冕。願保羅和哈巴安德牧師的榜樣激勵我們去回應神的呼召。

Lingnan University

Different articles in this collection refer to Christian education in China in the late 19th and the first half of the 20th century was illustrated under different contexts. That was a very active period for missionaries in China. One such account related to the republican revolution of 1911 and the Christian education of Dr. Sun, the founder of the Chinese republic. It was noted that a stronghold of the revolutionary insurgency was the Lingnan University in Canton. I would like to tell you more about this university which was founded by the American Presbyterian Church.

This paragraph is simply a translation of part of a paper presented by Professor Tze-ming Ng of the Hong Kong Minghua Theological College.

"Actually Christian education (in China) was not limited to the schools attended by Dr. Sun, of course. Other church affiliated schools were active in the revolution.

One was Lingnan which was not solely an evangelical school. Its aim was to develop character and to produce scientifically trained persons to meet Chinese needs. As its first Chinese president emphasized, Lingnan's purpose is to produce leaders for China who are equipped to use the sciences of the world; remove selfishness; benefit society; let the sense of responsibility shine forth as alumni of Lingnan. Professionalism and character building are contained in this Christian spirit, in step with the needs of the revolution. This compatibility formed the profound bond between Dr. Sun and Lingnan."

The first student ever to enroll at Lingnan was Chan Shiu-paak who later became a confidant of Dr. Sun; actually they became "blood" brothers in the Chinese sense. They swore their brotherhood. Chan epitomized the Lingnan spirit in his selfless service to the revolution. He desired no fame or glory and he turned down all offers of government appointments after the successful revolution. His famous quote became the golden saying of his generation, "Do great thing, seek no title". Today's China can certainly use this wisdom.

What was Christian education in the Chinese context? Lingnan's story tells us that Christian education is more than knowledge of the bible. It embraces all aspects of life, extending richly beyond the boundaries of the school.(John 10:10). True, some schools concentrated on evangelistic training, but most provided western ideas and ideals of civilization, science, and freedom. By this diversified front, the word of the bible is carried to all corners.

The example of Lingnan reminds us that spreading God's word is not always a frontal campaign. We can reach the heart and soul of the people around us in many ways.

嶺南大學

在前述的文章中，我們概括地了解到，19世紀末20世紀初，透過不同的處境，基督教在中國初現倪端。那是西方傳教士於中國最活躍的時期，與1911年民主革命和國父孫中山基督教教育之間發生千絲萬縷的關系。嶺南大學，一所被美國長老會認可的學府，是當時孫中山先生革命最強大的后盾之一。現將吳梓明教授所記載的一段歷史摘錄如下，此記載由香港明華神學院出版。

吳先生說，"基督教教育在中國，不僅局限於孫先生所逗留過的若干學校，其他學校眾多踴躍投入孫中山革命的人皆與教會有關。"

嶺南大學並非一間純碎傳道的學校。相反她的辦學宗旨是發展品格、培育具科學頭腦的人才、以回應當時中國的需要。嶺南的第一任中國校長曾經強調："嶺南大學的目的是提供世界级的科學教育，為中國培養領袖人才，從而鏟除自私，令社會得益。"嶺南精神所表達的是一種對社會的責任感，其專業和人格既體現著基督教的精神，又與革命的需要同步。這種互助、深邃的關系恰恰表達在孫中山與嶺南的關系上。

嶺南第一個簽名加入革命的學生名叫陳少白，他與孫中山不但成為結拜兄弟與至交，更成為嶺南精神的表率。他曾放棄所有名譽、光榮和政府頭銜，無私的將自己貢獻給孫中山革命。其至理名言"做大事、不求名"深為當時的時代所讚嘆,也當為今日中國所效法。

基督教教育對中國的意義在哪裡？嶺南的故事告訴我們，基督教教育不僅僅是有關聖經的知識，更是擁抱生命的每一個層面；基督教教育並不局限於校園，其所涉之処當更廣泛、更豐富……耶穌說，"我來了是要叫人得生命，並且得的更豐盛。"（約翰福音10:10)。

不錯，有些學校注重傳道的訓練，但更多中國的基督教學校，則是透過傳授西方的思想、文明、科學與自由的理念來培育學生。唯如此廣大和前瞻的胸襟，才能將聖經的話語和智慧發揮的更透徹、更深遠。

嶺南的故事告誡我們，無須正面交鋒，神的真理照樣可以透過不同的進路觸及人心。

She Who Never Stopped Giving: Charlotte Moon

Charlotte (Lottie) Moon came from a cultured southern background. A professor friend once remarked, "She writes the best English I have ever been privileged to read." She was educated at the Virginia Female Seminary and received an M.A. degree in classics at the Albemarle Female Institute, quite ahead of her times. She was appointed a missionary to China in 1872, breaking tradition for an unmarried woman. Her forty years in China produced a resounding response among Southern Baptists for missionary giving in her name, even today.

It would not be fruitful to trace her long labor for Christ step by step. I should like to only mention some highlights and inspiring quotations from this selfless evangelist who literally gave her life to the suffering people of northern China.

As an indication of the incredible difficulties of missionary work in China in that period, many colleagues fell into nervous prostration including her own sister who was never to recover.

Lottie's evangelism brought her to village visits, to enter homes to tell bible stories and to teach catechism and songs. She would sit cross-legged on the "kang" to talk to the women. A "kang" is an earthen bed heated by fire below, where the family ate and slept. "Foreign devils" were objects of curiosity. There was no privacy. As soon as the missionaries rose to eat breakfast, there would be spectators staring at them. A colleague commented to her, "Miss Moon, please note that we are being observed by thirty people; I have counted them."

Lottie answered, "Some boys are tearing holes in the paper windows. We are a wonderful sight, I suppose." Privately, she would write to a friend, "Have you ever felt the torture of human eyes bearing upon you, scanning every feature, every look, every gesture? I feel it keenly."

She spoke from early morning to late evening, from the kang, on the street, in the yard of dirty homes, in the heat and dust of summer or wintry rain and snow. Exposure to diseases was a certainty. Her only utterance, "I feel it is no idle fancy that the Master walks beside me, and I hear His voice saying gently, ' I am with you always, even unto the end.'" She found strength from the writing of Francis de Sales, "go on joyously as much as you can, and if you do not always go on joyously, at best go on courageously and confidently." Her dedication to God can be seen when she answered her niece who asked if she had ever been in love. "Yes, but God had first claim on my life, and since the two conflicted, there could be no question about the result."

Typically, no one spoke English where she worked. Loneliness was inescapable. Often she felt abandoned. She knew she was wearing herself out, but she adapted quickly and became totally native. Not only were living conditions challenging, persecution broke out in 1890. One of her churches faced destruction. She confronted the persecution leaders, "If you attempt to destroy this church, you will have to kill me first. Jesus gave Himself for us Christians. Now I am ready to die for Him." That impressed the mob.

One of her memorable sayings which is so relevant today: How many there are among our women, alas, who imagine that because "Jesus paid it all", they need pay nothing, forgetting that the prime object of their salvation was that they should follow in the footsteps of Jesus Christ! She was addressing women in stewardship. She was also quoted, "Now I honestly believe that I love China the best. Actually, which is stranger still, I love the Chinese best."

Famine and plague ravaged China in 1911. Lottie exhausted all her resources to help the sick and the indigent. She even stopped eating to give to the poor. Her strength failed. She weighed only fifty pounds and was taken on board a ship for America. She died on the way. Lottie Moon left us speechless.

施予無限----慕拉第

慕拉第，一個頗具美國南部色彩的名字。一位做學問的朋友曾說："她的文筆之優美令人刮目相看。" 慕拉第受教於維吉尼亞一所女子神學院，獲碩士學位，是美國南方最早獲此殊榮的女性之一。在美南浸信會放寬政策，准許單身女性到海外傳教後，她於1872年被差派進入中國。其後四十余年中國的服侍，令美南浸信會刻骨銘心。

慕拉第四十年中國服侍的記錄早已無從稽考。此文略為提及的，是這位無私的福音勇士為中國北方民眾作出的服侍與犧牲。

慕拉第時代，宣教事工在中國的艱辛程度實在無法用言語表達。此由其參與宣教事工的胞妹，健康在中國嚴重受損無法康復一事上可見一斑。

慕拉第事工的對象主要是中國北方農村。她到不同的村莊，進入各家各戶講述福音故事，做教義解答及教導聖詩頌唱，甚至她會盤腿坐在炕上對婦女們講道。炕，是中國北方舊時的大床，乃土坯與磚砌成的用膳及睡覺的長方台，炕上鋪墊草席，下面有孔道與煙囪相通，冬天可燒火取暖。炕上毫無隱私可言，因而睡在炕上的"洋鬼子"便會成為好奇的對象。傳教士每早起床用膳，四周都有圍觀的人群。有位同工曾對她說："慕小姐，我們睡覺的時候有三十個人在圍觀，我剛剛數過。" 慕拉第回答說："有些男孩子在窗紙上撕開個洞，朝著我們窺探呢。我想我們該是一道不錯的風景呢！" 她曾私下寫信給朋友說："你是否試過受眾人眼目鞭撻的情形？他們一寸一寸地掃視著你，每一個表情，每一個眼光，每一個姿態……我真切地感受到他們的眼神。"

每一天，從晨更到夜半，炕上、街上、民居骯髒的後院；酷熱多塵的暑天、刺骨雨雪的寒冬，慕拉第都在不間斷地教導，積勞成疾是必然的。然而她卻說："無可置疑，我的主一直與我同行，溫柔地說：'我必永遠與你同在，直到世界末了。'" 從聖方濟各·撒肋爵的著作裡，她得到能力："盡量喜樂！如果你不能常常喜樂，就盡可能勇敢並自信。" 慕拉第對 神全然擺上，當她的侄女問她是否曾經戀愛過的時侯，她說"是的，我曾經戀愛過。但唯有 神居我生命的首位，若兩者衝突，毫無疑問，結果祇有一個。"

很顯然，在她工作的地方，除她以外，再無他人能說英語。孤獨常伴左右，無可逃遁。她常常有被拋棄的感覺。她知道自己很疲累，但她竭力令自己適應環境，如土生一般融入當地的生活。然而，不僅是居住條件的惡劣，1890年，她更面對了一場不期然的迫害。她所建立的其中一所教會面臨摧毀。她勇敢地面對迫害者：“如果你試圖毀壞這座教堂，那你得先把我給殺了。耶穌曾為我們這些基督徒死，我現在也預備為祂殉道了。”凜然之言令暴徒震懾。

她的一句名言至今仍然發人深省：喂！在我們女子中，很多人覺得耶穌付上了一切代價，自己無需作什麼，卻忘記得救恩的關鍵，是跟隨基督耶穌的腳步！慕拉第教導婦女作主的門徒，指出：“現在，我深知中國是我的摯愛，我的確是個外人，但我深愛中國人。”

1911年，饑荒和瘟疫席捲中國，慕拉第傾盡所有幫助病患貧困之人，甚至為了給予窮人而不再進食。她的體力嚴重受損，體重降至五十磅，被送上返回美國的船隻，病逝於歸程。面对慕拉第忘我的人生，我們相形见拙，無言以對。

Wherefore China?

You might have read the story of a 20th century Presbyterian Jonah, John Leighton Stuart, a reluctant missionary to China, who stayed for 50 years. I hope that stirred your interest about the encounter of Christianity and China. What was the backdrop in that age which sent so many disciples of Christ to China? To test their Christian mettle? Even with premonition of martyrdom in some cases? Many of these dedicated men and women were the cream of their seminarian intelligentsia. They could have had outstanding careers at home as theologians, clergy, or university professors. Only the biographies of these saints can do justice to their obedience to God, each a saga of faith. Here, I wish only to set the stage for a select group who determined correctly that evangelism in company with modern education won souls most effectively.

Japan and China – Two Divergent Paths

We begin our story in the mid-19th century which saw the maturing of the industrial revolution in Europe. This led inexorably to the clash of cultures in Asia between the east and the west which took two diametrically opposite courses of development. The ever expanding appetites for markets and raw materials sent unwelcome waves which battered the imperial gates of China and Japan. While both ancient civilizations reacted with repulsion at first, Japan soon opened its doors and minds in its Meiji Restoration which rewarded with rapid development while China became the sick man of Asia in its attempts at isolationism. The collapse of the Ching Dynasty was followed by warlordism and civil war, coupled with Japanese invasion. China was left adrift.

Its educational system, even after the wrenching admission of failure in 1905, casting aside the ancient structure of veneration of classics to the exclusion of modernity, desperately needed infusion from liberal quarters, notably America. It was President Teddy Roosevelt who directed funds from the Boxer Indemnity to create momentum to educate students from China. I quote here from a learned source, "Chinese education was due for a radical change. Western science, technology, economy, politics, and perhaps morals, were insinuating themselves everywhere without invitation."

Missionary Influence in China's Universities & Beyond

Dr. Hu Shih, President of the National Peking University, 1931-37, made the following observation: The influence of the educational missionary has always been greater and more lasting and far-reaching than that of the evangelistic missionary. Attesting to this importance, in the 1930's, there were

16 Christian universities out of 56 universities and colleges in all of China. The educational missionaries performed feats, equivalents of which I have not come across in more recent history, in their width and depth of intellectual acumen. They not only learned many dialects of Chinese, they translated European and American literature, science, medicine, and law into Chinese. They produced dictionaries. Needless to say, they translated the Bible. Their valiant efforts in uniting the souls of Americans and Chinese despite separative forces of western political domination stood out as a patent commentary on the onerous dichotomy of the colonial times.

Their legacy were not only the universities of quality which became China's assets, but the spiritual sinews which in no small measure imbued the minds of revolutionaries like Dr. Sun Yat-sen. Mao Tsetung tried to denigrate the missionary endeavors, but there live on, in the minds and hearts of those who gave and of those who received, the memories of Christian love and teaching. Even today, we find alumni associations of China's Christian universities in America. The work of many lives has not been in vain.

何以中國？

或者在前面，你已經讀過我分享的20世紀的“約拿”---一個原本不欲涉足中國，卻最終將50年光陰奉獻給中國的傳教士司徒雷登的故事。我期望司徒雷登的故事能夠激發你對基督教與中國的興趣。那些年代，何以有如此多神的仆人被差往中國？幕后真相如何？是考驗他們委身基督的勇氣？抑或讓他們預嘗傳道的艱辛？許多獻身與宣教事業的男男女女，都曾是神學界知識分子的精英，在本國原本有機會成為杰出的神學家、神職人員、或大學教授，但因著對神的順服，秉行正義，他們譜寫了一曲曲信心傳奇的故事。此處，本文將透過一個小側面，來討論現代教育與傳福音的成功結合。

- 日本與中國---背道而馳的雙方

19世紀中葉歐洲工業革命日趨成熟，不可避免地導致了亞洲東西文化的碰撞，造成了兩個全然相反的發展路向。不斷擴充市場及原材料的欲望洶涌澎湃地撞擊著中國和日本的大門。雖說都是排外的文明古國，當中國堅持閉關自守，成為東亞病夫的時候，日本迅即開放門戶，施行明治維新，帶來了突飛猛進的發展與回報。很快中國清廷崩潰，之後軍閥割據、國民內戰，日本入侵令國家雪上加霜，中國變得漂泊無依。

1905年，排斥現代模式的中國舊教育制度，被認為是失敗的體制，極需灌輸美國開明的新思想。羅斯福總統利用庚子賠款資金，營造聲勢，訓練中國留學生。如學者所雲：“中國教育急需徹底改變。無論中國是否歡迎，西方的科學、技術、經濟、政治、甚至道德正逐步浸淫到中國的各個領域。”

- 傳教事業對中國大學及社會的影響

至於傳教士如何影響中國的教育與社會，國立北平大學校長胡適博士曾發表過如下觀察。他說：傳教士對中國教育的影響，遠甚於純粹的傳教，其影響更深遠更持久。的確如此，1930年全中國56所大學和學院中，基督教大學佔了16所。無論深度還是廣度，傳教士在學術方面的卓越貢獻，至今無人匹敵。傳教士不僅學習中國方言，亦將歐美文學、科學、醫藥及法律翻譯成中文。他們出版不同的字典，無需贅言，當然包括聖經。 與傳教士所在國的意願相反，他們不顧殖民地時代中美之間的二元劃分，力排雙方的離析和障礙，義無反顧地致力於中西精神的聯合。

傳教士遺留給中國的寶貴的資產，不僅僅是高質素、著名的大學，更是一種攝人心魄的力量，這種力量浸淫並影響著革命家孫中山博士及後來中國的國運。毛澤東試圖詆毀抹煞傳教士的貢獻，但傳教士的愛心、教導及影響將銘刻於所有受惠者的心中。即使今天，美國到處可見中國基督教大學的校友會。傳教士的貢獻並不徒然。

BIBLE INSIGHTS

讀經亮光

Bible or Gospel Accounts

Do you sometimes wonder about differences in the recording of events in the gospels? The four writers, Matthew, Mark, Luke, and John, for the most part were consistent. However, there are some differences. I refer to a few to illustrate. For example, John recorded some events and teachings that the other three (Synoptics) left out. Sometimes different details might emerge when the same event was being described.

In some cases, an event might be recorded in one gospel and ignored in another. John reported the wedding at Cana(John 2:1-12) when Jesus turned water into wine, while the others ignored it. You would think that such a miracle would be universally documented. We don't know why it was not. Like courtroom proceedings, different witnesses may give different accounts. Some witnesses may focus on different aspects of each event. Contradictions can also occur. Mark 5 and Luke 8 gave slightly different accounts of Jesus casting out demons from a man (two men?) who lived among the tombs. The question we should ask is, "Does it make any difference?" The point is that Jesus worked a miracle. Most of such differences do not change the essence of the report. The spirit of the events is not altered.

Sometimes, timing is inconsistent. When did Jesus drive out the merchants and money changers from the temple? The Synoptics differ from John again. In Matthew, Mark, and Luke, this happened close to the end of His public life, but John placed it near the beginning. Were there two such incidents? We don't know. We have to be mindful that the gospels have not reported all the deeds of Jesus.

There are also differences in the genealogies of Jesus. Matthew and Luke differ. Perhaps when they wrote, there was no absolutely reliable historical source available. The main point remains that Jesus was a descendant of David. For the followers of Christ, these numerical or chronological uncertainties are not critical. We are grateful that there are four gospels which add to our faith, with messages that flow in the same direction.

福音書記載的異同

你一定留意到，四本福音對某個事件的記錄，可能出入頗多。福音書的四位作者馬太、馬可、路加、約翰皆記載過許多相同的事件，但是記錄的方式各有迥異。舉例來說:

唯獨約翰福音提及迦拿婚宴上耶穌以水變酒　的神跡（約2：1-12），其他三本福音書則未有記載。

如同身處法庭的証人，供詞不同，記錄不同，甚至有時會出現矛盾。同樣，四福音書作者寫作的角度、手法亦有很大的不同與差異。　馬可福音5：與路加福音8：皆提及耶穌將鬼從那個住在墳塋中、滿有暴力的人身上趕出去。同樣的事件，馬太福音8：28-4的記錄就很不同。馬太認為有兩個人被鬼附身。　我們需要思考的是，四福音書彼此的差異，對今天基督徒的意義何在？我認為，耶穌的神跡發生在一個人身上，還是發生在兩個人身上並不重要，重要的是耶穌曾經以滿有憐憫的心，施行了神跡。

其次，四福音中在時間的問題上，各書的記錄並不吻合，互有差異。

耶穌何時趕出聖殿中買賣牛羊鴿子的人呢？前三福音認為，此事件發生在耶穌生命的尾聲；而約翰則認為是耶穌早期事工的年代。在耶穌的一生中，這個事件僅發生過一次呢？還是多次？無從稽考。

最後，有關耶穌的家譜。

作者以最好的記憶報告和描述了耶穌的家譜。而族譜源頭的知情人，非耶穌的養父約瑟莫屬。但是，當寫作的日子，約瑟經已過世，變得無從稽考，由此，馬太和路加的記錄明顯不同。

然而，族譜最重要的信息究竟是什麼？

最重要的信息是：耶穌基督是大衛的后裔、上帝的兒子。 四福音的記錄出自人手，自然存在出入，個別的細節，如時間、數字、年代的差異出入，非首要的考量。基督徒對上帝的信心，並非因時間、數字和年代而來。福音書作者最終的目的，乃是豐富我們的信仰，加強我們的信心。

How Is Peter Regarded?

Peter was one of the most important disciples and was often named first. Along with James and John, he was part of the inner circle of the twelve. The three of them were with Jesus in the garden of Gethsemane before the crucifixion. Totally not out of his own doing, he precipitated perhaps the most divisive controversy in all of Christendom. Did Christ anoint Peter as the foundation stone of the church? In other words, the head of the church.

Mathew 16:13-19. Jesus asked His disciples, "But what about you? Who do you say I am?" Simon Peter answered, "You are the Christ, the Son of the living God." Jesus replied, " Blessed are you, Simon son of Jonah, And I tell you that you are Peter, and on this rock I will build my church ...I will give you the keys of the kingdom of heaven...." The Catholic Church believes that this famous passage shows that Jesus made Peter the "prince of the apostles" and the foundation of the church. In addition, after Jesus asked Peter, "Do you love me?", "Feed my sheep" (John 21:17). Peter certainly appeared to be favored.

The Protestants disagree. They believe that Jesus meant building the church on what Peter said, not on Peter himself. They cite Acts 15. Paul and Barnabas brought the question of circumcision of Gentiles to the apostles in Jerusalem from Antioch. There was a debate between the Pharisees and the apostles. Peter was one of the apostles who spoke. At the end, James, the brother of the Lord, made the concluding remarks, "It is my judgment, therefore, that we should not make it difficult for the Gentiles who are turning to God....". James was in charge of the council, not Peter or Paul. This passage did not portray Peter as the head of the apostles in the Council of Jerusalem. Also Gal 2:8-9 recorded the division of ministry between Peter and Paul as well as Paul's rebuke of Peter. "For God, who was at work in the ministry of Peter as an apostle to the Jews, was also at work in my ministry as an apostle to the Gentiles. James, Peter, and John, those reputed to be pillars ... They agreed that we should go to the Gentiles, and they to the Jews." There is no hint that Peter was the anointed prince of the apostles. Moreover, Paul described how he confronted Peter for Peter's hypocrisy. These references do not support Peter's leading role.

The controversy is alive and well. Catholic tradition names Peter as the first bishop of Rome (Pope), but there is nothing in the Gospels to suggest that the first Christians thought there should be a "head bishop".

如何看彼得的職分？

彼得是主耶穌最重要的門徒之一，位居眾門徒之首，與雅各及約翰，被視為主耶穌最親近的門徒。他們三人也是主耶穌被釘十字架前，於客西馬尼園的同伴。可惜事與心違，在其身後，其職份在基督教圈子內產生了極大的分歧。果真是耶穌將教會建立在彼得這塊磐石上的嗎？換句話說，他果真是教會的頭嗎？

馬太16:13-19，耶穌問門徒，"你們說我是誰？"西門彼得回答說："你是基督，是永生神的兒子。"耶穌回答說："西門巴約拿，你是有福的，我告訴你，你是彼得，在這磐石上，我要建立我的教會......將天國的鑰匙給你......"

天主教會認為,這段著名的經文表明了耶穌曾賜予彼得使徒"王子"和教會根基的身份。此外，耶穌還問彼得："你愛我嗎？"，"你餵養我的羊。"（約翰福音21:17）。彼得確實為耶穌所器重。

新教徒卻不以為然。他們認為，耶穌將教會建造在磐石上的意思，是指彼得所宣稱的話，而非指彼得本人。新教徒引用使徒行傳15章，保羅和巴拿巴自安提阿將外邦人是否當行割禮的問題帶給耶路撒冷使徒，法利賽人和使徒之間展開辯論，彼得在當中發言。辯論結束時，耶穌的兄弟雅各，歸納總結了這次辯論，他說，"諸位弟兄，請聽我的話。方才西門述說神當初怎樣眷顧外邦人，從他們中間選取百姓歸於自己的名下；眾先知的話也與這意思相合。正如經上所寫的：此後，我要回來，重新修造大衛倒塌的帳幕，把那破壞的重新修造建立起來，叫餘剩的人，就是凡稱為我名下的外邦人，都尋求主。這話是從創世以來，顯明這事的主說的。所以據我的意見，不可難為那歸服神的外邦人；......"。非彼得或保羅，　乃雅各負責主持了是次耶路撒冷議會。此議會未曾提及彼得就是耶路撒冷眾使徒的頭。

加拉太書2:8-9記錄彼得和保羅之間的分歧，保羅責備彼得"那感動彼得、叫他為受割禮之人作使徒的，也感動我，叫我為外邦人作使徒；又知道所賜給我的恩典，那稱為教會柱石的雅各、磯法、約翰，就向我和巴拿巴用右手行相交之禮，叫我們往外邦人那裡去，他們往受割禮的人那裡去。"

此処沒有任何跡象顯示彼得被膏立為使徒之首，保羅描述彼得裝假的引述，皆不支持彼得的領導地位。

爭議依然存在，有爭議是好的。天主教的傳統認為，彼得曾是羅馬教廷的第一位主教（教宗），但福音書卻從未提及初代基督徒認為教會應該有一個“首主教”。

Indebted to Thomas

Does doubt come to mind when we think of Thomas? We must be careful in using the word, doubt. When doubt arises from vicious living, leading to uncertainty about God, doubt is blame-worthy. The careless and the foolish also face doubt when life nears its end. Specifically, their indifference to the Christian message gives rise to this kind of doubt. They have not tried to know Christ. Such doubts should not be confused with honest doubt, the doubt that issues from the depth of sincere and thoughtful hearts. This is a noble doubt while the former is base and unholy.

John 20:27-28. "Then He said to Thomas,' Put your finger here, see my hands. Reach out your hand and put it into my side. Stop doubting and believe.' Thomas said to him, ' My Lord and my God.' "

The unbelief of Thomas has made us richer. It shows that the disciples were not credulous simpletons, willing to believe anything without discernment. Thomas, unwittingly, testified to the Resurrection of Jesus. Jesus knew that the doubt of Thomas was not an excuse to reject His victory over death. The truth in Jesus' resurrection commands soulful scrutiny. It is the most important event in all of history. No one can blame Thomas for his doubt. Jesus did not. He was kind to Thomas. Maybe Thomas was a rationalist among the disciples who was unable to believe things he could not see or touch. His eyes were not sufficient; he had to touch. His doubt was intelligible considering the supreme importance of the claim. He had only the evidence of ten men in opposition to the evidence of all time. No one had come back from the grave. Nothing would have given him greater delight than to be assured that his master was alive. We can see his joy when he shouted, "My Lord and my God!" The memory of Calvary convinced him that his master was dead. His doubt was honest.

Thomas not only found proof for all the countless generations of believers, he was the reason that Jesus said, "Thomas, because thou hast seen me, thou hast believed: blessed are they that have not seen, and yet have believed." The significance of these words is that Jesus was saying them to us. We have not seen Jesus's wounds. We have the harder challenge, and therefore the more glorious part. We are indeed indebted to Thomas who brought about more blessedness for us.

多亏有多馬！

當腦海裏浮現出多馬的時候，我們會否聯想到他的懷疑呢？

請慎用"懷疑" 一詞。因敗壞的生活，導致不肯定、懷疑上帝是當受指責的。生命臨近終結，對基督教的信息冷漠、粗心；愚頑之人不嘗試認識基督，反倒產生懷疑。這種懷疑不當與誠實的、發自內心深處的疑問相提並論，后者乃高尚的疑問，與前者出於邪惡的懷疑不可同日而語。

約翰福音20:27-28記載，耶穌對多馬說，" 伸 過 你 的 指 頭 來 ， 摸 我 的 手 ； 伸 出 你 的 手 來 ， 探 入 我 的 肋 旁 。 不 要 疑 惑 ， 總 要 信 。多 馬 說 ： 我 的 主 ！ 我 的 神 ！"

不信的多馬豐富了我們。讓我們知道，門徒們並不是不經鑒別、全盤照收的傻瓜。多馬，不知不覺中，證明了耶穌的復活。耶穌了解多馬的懷疑不是一個不信的藉口，不是要抗拒祂那勝過死亡的勝利。耶穌復活的真理實在需要深情款款的推敲，因為它是整個歷史中最重要的事件。多馬的懷疑無可指責，耶穌非但不指責他，待他卻甚為友善。門徒中，或許托馬斯是個理性主義者，不能夠相信那些未曾聽見、未曾接觸的事物。他的眼睛不滿足於看見，他要親自接觸。他懷疑，他要理智地考慮有關復活這個宣稱的重要性。

髑髏地的記憶說，他的主死了，他的疑問是誠實的。除了這十個門徒以外，再無任何證據表明此事件的真實性，沒有一個人能從墳墓裏出來，也沒有任何事情能帶給他更大的喜悅。面對復活的恩主，他高聲喊着："我的主，我的神！"的時候，他的喜悅是溢于言表的。

多馬，為歷代信徒見證了主的復活。但是，耶穌對他說："多馬，你 因 看 見 了 我 才 信 ； 那 沒 有 看 見 就 信 的 有 福 了 。"耶穌的話之所以重要，是因為祂要所有的基督徒都聽見這句話。對于從未見到耶穌釘痕的我們来說，當中的挑戰更甚，也更榮耀。實在說來，要感謝為我們帶來諸多福份的多馬。

The People Israel

As the twelfth century B.C. opened, Egypt and the Hittite Empire were going under. The power struggle in western Asia exhausted all the contesting nations. A wave of migration by the "People of the Sea" appeared down the Syrian coast into the land of Canaan. These became known as Canaanites or Amorites, a Semitic people of Palestine and Syria. They shared Northwest-Semitic elements with the ancestors of the Israelites. It was near this time that exodus occurred and the subsequent conquest of Canaan by the Jews. Therefore, the dominant pre-Israelite population was in race and language not different from Israel. Some non-Semitic peoples also shared the land. A brilliant achievement of Canaan culture was its writing alphabet which passed to Phoenicia and Greece, and eventually to Western Europe. Literacy accompanied the age of Israel's origins.

Canaanite religion was, however, a very different picture. Baal Ashtaroth worship comprised bloodthirsty practices, sacred prostitution, and sexual rites. These were repugnant to the Jews.

Israel as a people stepped onto the world stage given this setting. To understand better the process of the conquest and the subsequent developments, it is helpful to trace the formation of the People Israel as they evolved from Egyptian slavery to nationhood in Canaan. We must resist the temptation to oversimplify history by assuming that twelve sons of Jacob, with their families, went down into Egypt and became the large number who exited with Moses, capturing Palestine after wandering in the desert. The bible offers evidence that the people of Israel was formed by a complex process, absorbing and amalgamating with very diverse tribes.

First of all, all the ancestors of the later Israel could not have participated in the exodus. The number of men, about 600,000, would mean something like two to three million in all. Seventy men and their families could not multiply into this large number in that time frame. We must not take the biblical number literally. Only two midwives served the group, so the number had to be much smaller. (Ex. 1:15-22). A few thousand would be reasonable. This leads to the conclusion that all of later Israel could not have descended from them exclusively. During their time of slavery, many other peoples joined their ranks, Egyptians, Midianites, Amalekites, Kenizzites, etc.. The Egyptian overlords were not too particular.

Even during their journey in the wilderness, miscellaneous groups joined them, becoming converts, so to speak. The incompleteness of the conquest also means that many Canaanite peoples were incorporated later. (Judges 1:21, 2 Sam. 5:6-10). There were even components of Israel living in

Canaan before the conquest. No doubt, Israel absorbed kindred people already present in the land who had not participated in exodus or conquest. So, the eventual shape of the Israelite genealogy was formed after the settlement in Palestine. It was not a linear development from Jacob.

Now that we have reviewed briefly the formation of the People Israel, what can we say about being God's chosen people? God did not require a "pure" race, but God required a common purpose and purity of spirit. We Chinese are sometimes guilty of regarding ourselves as a pure race, often the Han. In fact, China is a mixture of many peoples. The unity or purity we must seek is the word of God. We have been incorporated into the New Israel.

In this article, I am trying to say how the Israelites mixed with other peoples from the time of slavery to settlement in Canaan. They were not purely the descendants from Jacob. The conclusion is that God does not require purity in race but purity in spirit. We are the people of God and consist of mixtures of people who are the new Israel.

以色列人

公元前12世紀，埃及與赫梯帝國日趨衰微，權力相爭消耗了西亞所有臣屬國家的國力。隨後興起的海上移民浪潮由敘利亞海岸直達迦南地。而這些移民便是巴勒斯坦與敘利亞稱為閃米特人的迦南人和亞摩利人。他們與以色列祖先們一同分享了西亞北非閃族的文明。而這種文明與當時逃出埃及、定居迦南的以色列人的文化相距甚近。非閃族人與后來的以色列人在種族及語言上沒有什麼明顯的不同，故而他們共同分享著其中的土地。迦南文化輝煌的成就，影響著後來的腓尼基、希臘的文字，乃至西歐文化。它伴隨著以色列的文化漸趨成熟。

值得一提的是，迦南人的宗教則是一幅迥異的畫面。巴力亞斯他錄崇拜的嗜血殘忍、淫穢、和生殖崇拜，都令以色列人極為厭惡。

作為一個民族，以色列人開始步入歷史舞台。了解其南征北戰及之后發展的歷史，將有助於我們了解這個由埃及出來定居迦南的民族形成的過程。我們需要非常小心，不要簡化這段歷史，以為這就是雅各與其12個兒子及其家人下埃及，成為人數眾多的族群；之后與摩西一同經過曠野漂泊，進入巴基斯坦的歷史。聖經上有証據表明，以色列民族的形成是個復雜的過程，當中吸收並融合著許多不同的部落和族群。

首先，進入迦南地的以色列祖先幾乎都沒有參與出埃及的事件。從當時出埃及的男人大約60萬，即可推測出總人數可能為2-3百萬人，與聖經所錄70個男人和其家庭人數對比相當懸殊。以其定居的年限來看，他們根本無法繁衍出如此龐大的人群。我們不當僅僅從字面上理解聖經的數字。當時為奴之地祇有兩個收生婆為以色列人接生，所以實際的數字可能要小得多（出1:15-22），幾千人的說法較為合理。

綜括而言，後來的以色列人並不都出於最初的族系，其后裔未必是絕對純粹的后裔。

在以色列被奴役的日子，很多異族加入到他們當中，包括埃及人、米甸人、亞馬利人、基尼人等，所有這些人都處於埃及的統治之下。可以說，即使在曠野的旅途中，仍然有外族人不斷皈依，加入到他們當中。由於以色列人未能完全征服迦南地，導致後來很多迦南的原居民也混雜當中（士1:21;撒上5:6-10），毫無疑問，以色列一直處於一個吸納人口的狀態中，無論是出埃及時期還是爭戰時期，所以，以色列族譜最終的形態是定居巴勒斯坦之后形成的，並非由雅各一支單線沿襲下來的。

至此，我們已經簡要地回顧了以色列民族形成的過程，他們並非出自雅各一脈。由此可見，上帝所看中的，未必是族類的“純正”，上帝需要的是一致的目標及純正的精神。我們就是被上帝接納的新以色列人。

Israel and Judah

When the Israelites settled down in Palestine after exodus, twelve tribes which occupied assigned geographic areas were loosely joined in a confederation overseen by "Judges". There was no strong centralized leadership. The social and economic system was changing from nomadic to agricultural. Also they felt a need to defend against unfriendly neighbors. This called for a centralized government. They invented a constitutional monarchy whose kings were not descendants of God. The Jewish kings were accountable to God's laws. King Solomon increased the central power at the expense of tribal authority through taxation. However, the country had always been politically polarized in a northern portion with ten tribes, Israel, and a southern portion with two tribes, Judah.

Both David and Solomon of Judah were wise enough to seek the consent of Israel for their rule over both Israel and Judah. When Solomon died in 922 B.C., his son Rehoboam succeeded him. When he went to Shechem in Israel to be crowned, the leaders of Israel met him to ask for more lenient taxation. He refused to listen to advice of moderation and conciliation. His arrogant ways caused the rift between Israel and Judah. In the northern kingdom of Israel, dynasties came and went in rapid succession. A critical point changed the course of Israel. Jezebel, a Sidonite princess, became queen. This notorious woman, armed with missionary zeal for her cult of Baal, subjected her adopted land to religious strife. Even though she was eventually overthrown, the seeds of paganism were replanted in the kingdom. The prophet, Elisha, helped ousting Jezebel.

An inner perversion of Israel's faith had taken place. Religious decay went hand in hand with social sickness. Extreme contrast between rich and the poor racked the country. Political dysfunction marked the declining years. Kings were murdered in quick order, plunging the country into civil war. The rising Assyrians Empire made its move. Some of the citizens were deported, giving rise to the idea of the "lost tribes" of Israel. Only Judah and Benjamin in the southern kingdom remained intact. The "lost tribes" were Asher, Dan, Ephraim, Gad, Issachar, Manasseh, Naphtali, Reuben, Simon, and Zebulun. Levi was probably among the lost tribes, but it was not one of the "landed" tribes and was not specifically mentioned.

There is some controversy regarding the identity and degree of disappearance of these tribes. Speculation abounds on the question of their possible eventual reunion with Judah. Many diverse people have claimed to be descendants of the lost tribes. They range in locations from Africa, the Middle East, the Far East, to even England and America. Most likely these people gradually merged into Assyrian society. The Assyrians not only conquered

Israel but also brought foreigners to settle there. The resulting mix of people was known as Samaritans who were not well regarded by the Jews of the south, on account of their genealogy and religious dilution. One interesting question might be asked regarding the different outcomes of ethnic survival contrasting Israel with Judah in their respective national defeats.

Judah managed to survive even as Israel in the north vanished into history because Judah at first paid tribute to Assyria and became a vassal state. Late in the 7th century B.C., Assyria itself was collapsing and was finished in year 609 B.C.

Judah became independent by default. King Josiah launched a sweeping reform and even recovered some provinces of Israel. The reform aimed to repudiate the Assyrian cult and to purge idolatrous practices. By coincidence, "the book of the law", a form of Deuteronomy, was found in the course of repairing the Temple of Jerusalem. This book of the law strengthened the whole reform movement. The Davidic line and Yahweh's covenant were affirmed. A return to ancient tradition was stressed. Judgment was in the air. Prophets were saying that the wrath of Yahweh was imminent if the nation did not repent. Zephaniah and Jeremiah lent much sympathy for Josiah's political and religious policy.

A lingering problem was the fact that the reform tended to be satisfied with external measures which might not have affected the spiritual life of the nation, creating a false sense of peace. Jeremiah complained that it had produced nothing but increased cultic activity without real return to ancient paths. (Jer. 6:16-21)

In due course, Babylonia put an end to Judah. How did the Jews survive as a people when the Israelites of the north did not? It was in no small part due to Jeremiah and Ezekiel. They prepared the people as individuals under Yahweh's covenant law in place of the national cult.

They stressed internal cleansing (Jer.4:3), preparing for the day when religion would have to go on without external cult at all, such as in exile. They assured the people that Yahweh would meet them, without temple and without cult, in the land of their captivity if they sought Him with their whole heart. (Jer. 29:11-14, Ezek. 11:16)

The inscription of the law in their hearts sustained the Jews so that they did not vanish in exile and persecution. They waited for God's redemptive act. I hope this very brief scan of the life cycle of Israel has removed some of the mystery of Jewish history.

以色列和猶大

出埃及後，在巴勒斯坦分地而居的以色列十二個支派，缺乏強有力的中央政權統一管治，鬆散地聯合於"士師"的監督之下。社會與經濟體制由遊牧業向農業過渡。為抵禦不友善的鄰邦，他們認為建立中央集權政府迫在眉睫。然而猶太人的國王須對上帝的律法負責，一個君主立憲制的王國並不是神的心意。為鞏固中央集權，所羅門王通過稅收的手段削弱各支派的力量。最終政治格局分化為北國以色列的十個支派與南國猶大的兩個支派。

南國猶大的大衛與所羅門以其睿智，尋得北國以色列的支持，獲取了聯合王國的治權。公元前922年，所羅門王死後，其子羅波安繼位。於示劍接受加冕之時，以色列眾首領尋求他在稅收方面的寬容，遭其拒絕，羅波安的傲慢導致了南北關係的破裂，最終分裂成為兩個國家。北國以色列朝代更迭頻繁，某個關鍵時期更令北國國運急轉直下。聲名狼藉的外邦的公主耶洗別成為以色列國的王后，並以其極大的熱情崇拜假神巴力，導致宗教衝突。雖然她最終被推翻，但是異教崇拜的種子深植以色列民心。先知以利沙曾竭力根除耶洗別所造成的影響。

信念的歪曲在民眾內心產生影響，宗教沉淪與社會腐化同時加深。貧富懸殊加速了國力的頹勢，篡權奪勢成為以色列暮年的主調，君王的連番遇害，更導致國家陷入內戰狀態。新興的亞述帝國導致國家崩潰，部分以色列民被擄遷移，除猶大與便雅憫支派得以倖存外，"失落的支派"成為一個長久的話題。他們包括亞設、但、以法蓮、迦得、以薩迦、瑪拿西、拿弗他利、流便、西緬和西布倫。利未支派或屬於其中一個失落的支派，因其不擁有土地，所以未特別提及。

曾有一些討論，題及十個支派消失的程度。至於他們最終如何回歸、與猶大重聚，則有層出不窮的猜測。很多散居於非洲、中東、遠東，甚至英倫及美洲的人，稱自己為失落支派的後裔。這些失縱的支派，最大的可能是他們逐步融入了當時的亞述社會。亞述人不僅征服了以色列，也將大量外邦人遷入以色列定居，結果產生了倍受猶大南國歧視的撒瑪利亞雜族，這些族群的出現稀釋了以色列的族系與信仰。有趣的是，南北存亡形成鮮明對比，當北國逐漸湮沒於歷史長河之時，猶大卻藉著進貢亞述而成為其附庸國，得以成功地生存下來。公元前7世紀，隨著亞述亡國，猶大重新成為獨立國家。

當時的約西亞王實施大規模的改革，甚至恢復了以色列的某些省份。改革的目的主要是清除偶像崇拜。巧合的是，在耶路撒冷聖殿的維修中律法書被發現。此書的出現推動了整個改革運動。“大衛之約” 及古老的傳統得以重申和強調，審判氛圍凝重。先知呼籲國家悔改，強調耶和華的忿怒已迫在眉睫。先知西番雅和耶利米對於約西亞王的政治與宗教政策傾注了同情。

然而，約西亞王的改革僅僅流於表面，營造的祇是一個虛假祥和的氛圍，並未在精神層面對國家產生實質的影響，積重難返的偶像崇拜依然存在。先知耶利米曾經抱怨說，改革徒俱虛表，並未帶領民眾真正回歸古老律法書的要求。（耶6:16-21）

巴比倫帝國興起消滅猶大南國，民眾被擄至巴比倫。較之北國的消亡殆盡，作為族群的南國猶大如何得以倖存呢？先知耶利米和以西結功不可沒。他們教導民眾瞭解，與耶和華所立的約，不是徒有外表的集體崇拜，對上帝的崇拜亦是個人的。

先知們在國家流亡的日子預備人心，強調人心的清潔（耶4：3），讓國民知道，若他們專心尋求耶和華，守耶和華的律法，即使失去聖殿，也必能與神相遇。由於此信念深入人心，在被擄之地遭遇流放與迫害之時，他們仍然能夠等候上帝的救贖。(耶29:11-14;結11:16)

期盼透過對以色列族群發表的管窺之見，得以解開猶太人某些歷史之謎。

Jonah by Another Name

The Old Testament's Jonah was not a Presbyterian, but a famous Presbyterian of the 20th Century was a Jonah.

Most of us have heard about Jonah and Nineveh, but there is often another meaning of Nineveh in our lives. It is an insufferable task ordained by the Almighty. It may be something, some place, or some person that we desperately want to avoid. It is not only inconvenient, but wholly distasteful.

John Leighton Stuart was a Presbyterian, born in China, of missionary parents. He spent his early years in Hangzhou near Shanghai. He became more Chinese than I can claim to be. He, as an adult, spoke Mandarin, and the dialects of Hangzhou, Ningpo, and Shanghai. Although he was brought up as a blue-blooded Christian, his view of missionary work in China was abhorrent. In his own words, "it is difficult to exaggerate the aversion I had developed against going to China as a missionary." He continued to describe the evangelistic scene at the end stage of the Ching Dynasty as "haranguing crowds of idle, curious people in street chapels or temple fairs, selling tracts (religious pamphlets) for almost nothing, being regarded with amused or angry contempt by the native population, physical discomforts or hardships, etc., ... a sort of living death..."

Despite a choice Christian college education at Hampden-Sydney College, a ranking school of the era, and graduate studies at Union Theological Seminary of Virginia, he admitted to being unenthusiastic towards missionary service (in China). The congenial life and the opportunity for scholarly pursuit in Virginia were too inviting. He developed a violent reaction against foreign missions as a career, but woe be to him, The Student Volunteer Movement for Foreign Missions was beginning to accelerate, reaching the flood tide. His outstanding school record made him a target of recruitment. It was almost axiomatic that any sincere Christian young man or woman must show why he should not answer the call to be a foreign missionary. He wore Jonah's sandals and they agonized him. He tried to bury himself in teaching Latin and Greek, the subjects he loved. His parents never put pressure on him to be a missionary, but he could hear God's call even as he tried to "run away."

One fateful night, he lay awake and counted the clock tower bell ringing the hours until 5 am while the questions of faith and sacrifice grilled him. Finally, he decided to put his religious belief to the ultimate test. He would decide to be a missionary and have the satisfaction of proving to himself that Christianity was for him the ultimate value. If God knew that he could not meet the demands of life in China, he would trust God to lead him elsewhere. He then fell asleep.

Next day, he told his closest friends who were not surprised. Maybe they knew a Jonah when they saw one.

John Leighton Stuart later became a professor of New Testament Literature and Exegesis at the Nanking Theological Seminary.

He wrote an authoritative *Greek-Chinese-English Dictionary of the New Testament* and was instrumental in establishing the Yenching University in Peking, and was its first president. He was appointed as ambassador to China by President Truman in 1946. His ashes now rest in China at his request.

We may have our "John Leighton Stuart's" in our church. Let them hear God's call and answer in their own ways.

又名約拿的司徒雷登

舊約中的先知約拿并非長老宗會友，但有一位20世紀的約拿則是一位知名的長老宗會友。那麼，他是誰呢？

舊約約拿與尼尼微的故事家喻戶曉，但尼尼微在我們生命中或者有另一種隐喻----或許是全能者授予的艱巨任務，或許是我們極欲逃避的某事、某人、甚至某些地方；總之，尼尼微是個令人乏味、憹惡的稱謂。

司徒雷登，美國長老會會友，生於中國，其父母均為在華傳教士。早年生活於臨近上海的杭州城渡過，是個名副其實的中國通，不僅通曉國語，且深諳當地方言，如杭州話、寧波話和上海話。作為一個傳統的基督徒，對於在中國宣教，他曾甚為抵觸。借用他自己的話說："對於在中國作傳教士的厭惡，我是無法用言語訴說得清楚的。"清朝末期的宣教情形被他描述為："空虛無聊的高談闊論者，廟會街上好奇的人們，賣不出去的福音單張和小冊子，傳教士備受當地人譏笑謾罵，身體困苦不適……，簡直生不如死！"

儘管司徒雷登受教並畢業於頂尖的基督教學校和神學院，但他坦承對於去中國宣教瞭無熱誠，沉溺於維吉尼亞愜意學者生活的他，甚至極力反對海外宣教。但　神的眷顧還是臨到了他。隨著海外宣教學生運動的蓬勃興起，運動的浪潮開始席捲而入。出色的學術成就令其成為征尋的對象。他迫於壓力，卻極不情願，於是便埋首於摯愛的拉丁文和希臘文的教授工作。他的父母從未對他參與宣教施以壓力，然而，無論如何逃避，神的呼召還是臨到了他。

這是一個決定命運的夜晚。午夜，司徒雷登醒來，信仰和獻身的問題彷如鐘樓裏的鐘錘，一下一下地撞擊著他，直到凌晨5點。終於，他決定來個破釜沉舟，通過參與宣教，去證明基督教信仰對他是否真的具有至高無上的價值。如果　神認為他不能承受在中國的生活，他相信 神對他將另有安排。想到此，他再度安然入睡。

第二天，他將這一切告知好友，而他們並不感到意外。或許，他們早已看見了那個順服的約拿。

後來，司徒雷登不僅成為南京金陵神學院的新約文學與釋經學教授，撰寫了極具權威的《新約希漢英大字典》，他還奠定了燕京大學（現北京大學）的根基，且榮任燕京第一任校長。1946年，他被美國杜魯門總統任命為美國駐華大使。離世後，骨灰被送返中國，葬於杭州某處。

在我們的教會裏，相信有許許多多的司徒雷登。請你用心聆聽神的呼召，並且予以回應！

Mary Magdalene

How did the traditional belief that Mary Magdalene was a reformed prostitute come about? There is actually no concrete support in the Gospels for this assumption. Popular culture has reinforced this idea in such famous shows as Jesus Superstar. The Gospels tell us that Jesus cast out seven demons from her (Mark 16:9, Luke 8:2).

Luke 7:36-50 tells of a dinner where a "woman who had lived a sinful life" anointed Jesus's feet with perfume, weeping all the while. Jesus' host protested that Jesus did not object. On the contrary, Jesus explained that "her many sins have been forgiven--for she has loved much." He told the woman, "Your faith has saved you; go in peace." Her name was never mentioned. Tradition connected her with Mary Magdalene. Another Mary, the sister of Lazarus, also anointed Jesus' feet with perfume. Judas Iscariot took exception to this waste of expensive perfume.

Even though Mary Magdalene's demons were cast out by Jesus, we have no reason to believe she had been a prostitute. Uncertainty further arises when Luke's Gospel mentioned Mary Magdalene by name in other places but did not do so at the occasion of anointing Jesus's feet.

Whether Mary Magdalene was or was not a prostitute does not affect our faith. It has to do with how we read the Bible. We don't want to invent "truths".

抹大拉的馬利亞

抹大拉的馬利亞是個被改變的妓女，如此傳統說法由何而來？

事實上，福音書對這種假設並沒有具體的支持，祇是透過流行文化，及欣賞表演耶穌的電影名星，這種假設得以普及和強化。福音書告訴我们的，是耶穌從這個馬利亞身上趕出七個鬼（馬可福音16:9，路加福音8:2）。

路加福音7:36-50講述了一個活在罪中的女人，在最后的晚餐上，哭泣著用香膏膏耶穌的腳。用晚餐那間屋子的主人對此備感詫異-----為什麼耶穌不拒絕罪人？　耶穌說，因為她的愛多，所以她許多的罪都被赦免了　。耶穌對那個女人說，“你的信救了你，平平安安的回去吧。”傳統認為，這就是抹大拉的馬利亞。

另一個馬利亞，即拉撒路的姐姐，也曾膏過耶穌的腳，加略人猶大曾責備說，她枉然浪費了昂貴的香膏。

耶穌曾從抹大拉的馬利亞身上將鬼趕出去，即使如此，也毫無理由說她就是一名妓女。同樣，路加福音也曾提及抹大拉馬利亞的名字，但並非膏抹耶穌腳的場合。

抹大拉的馬利亞是否妓女一事，不當影響我們的信心，關鍵在於我們當如何讀經---相信聖經是神所默示的話？還是一味在經文中鑿作“真相”。

Are Kings Better Than God?

The Israelites wanted a king like their neighboring nations. Monarchy started with Saul. Then came David and Solomon. Soon came the end of the united nation. Why? Kings are only human even if anointed by prophets. The Israelites were actually warned but they did not listen.

Most people know the heroic story of David and Goliath, but how many know that the fugitive David offered his services to the Philistines and became a vassal to the Philistine king of Gath, out of reach from Saul. In due course, Saul died at the hands of the Philistine army. David was spared involvement in Saul's death because the Philistines did not trust him to take the field against his own people.

David became king of Judah with the consent of the Philistines. His rule spanned several tribes, but Judah crowned him without consultation with all the tribes of Israel. A surviving son of Saul actually contested his rule. Much political intrigue and bad blood preceded the unification of Israel under David. The northern part of the country was Saul's territory and it grudgingly submitted to the king of Judah. Sectional jealousies remained. David's military skills obtained for him independence from the Philistines. He had the wisdom to choose Jerusalem as the new capital, being centrally located and not part of any tribal land. The city was David's own holding which he conquered with his personal troops, to be known as "The City of David". He made Jerusalem the political as well as the religious capital for this people. This helped him bind the north and south together. What is less noticed is that the state displaced the tribes gradually and inexorably.

Israel was committing to the idea of a monarchy chiefly on the accomplishment of David. However, the seeds of division were planted when the problem of succession arose. There was much jealousy and hatred among David's sons by different mothers. On the strength of palace intrigue, Solomon was made David's heir. He proceeded to consolidate his power by ruthlessly killing all possible contenders, not very godly conduct.

Solomon's economic prosperity was achieved at the great costs. One price paid was an increase in the power of the state and a taxation burden to be regretted later. He resorted to the hated corvee, the compulsory labor for the state. He also used slave labor extensively. Was this God's intention?

The most far-reaching change in the fabric of society was the displacement of tribal confederacy with its sacral institutions and charismatic leadership, by the dynastic state. God's original plan was deformed. Tribal independence came to an end. The effective basis of social obligation was no longer God's covenant, but state power.

In the north, some objected to the principle of dynastic succession and rejected the idea of perpetual rule by the Davidic house. Many objected to the tyranny of Solomon. There was always tension and divisiveness.

Therefore, it was no accident that the nation split when Solomon died. His son, Rehoboam, brought about the schism by his arrogance and stupidity in dealing with the long suffering northerners. Soon the divided kingdom, Israel and Judah, became second rate powers. Assyria and Babylonia put an end to these kingdoms which were ruled mostly by evil minded rulers in murderous succession.

The lesson we learn is that when the chosen people turned away from God and depended on their own devices, corruption followed. The wisest kings could not tend the course with God. Ps.146:3-5 reminds us, "Do not put your trust in princes, in mortal men, who cannot save. When their spirit departs, they return to the ground, on that very day their plans come to nothing. Blessed is he whose help is the God of Jacob."

君王？上帝？

如同四周的鄰國一般，以色列人希望擁有自己的國王。

王國時代始於掃羅，之後是大衛、所羅門......旋即到了聯合王國的尾聲。

何故如此？盡管君王皆由先知膏立，但是他們都是人；以色列人早已得此警告，可惜他們充耳不聞。

大衛對抗歌利亞的英雄故事可謂街知巷聞。但是又有多少人曉得，逃亡的大衛曾經投靠於非利士人麾下。掃羅死於腓利士軍隊之手，於大衛無關，全因非利士人的不信任，致使他免上戰場，骨肉相殘。

大衛後來成為猶太王，管轄以色列的多數支派，但是加冕為王未能知照以色列的所有支派。掃羅的後裔同樣垂涎角逐王位。政治謀略、殺害和宮廷斗爭在大衛登基、王國統一前已經存在。北方原屬掃羅的領地，服從南方的猶太王純屬無奈，地方嫉妒屢見不鮮。

大衛的軍事手段令他成功地獨立於非禮士人之外，他帶兵攻克位於南北中心地帶的耶路撒冷，並智慧的選擇其為首都，使之不隸屬任何支派。耶城既是政治宗教的中心，又助他將南北兩國聯合，乃眾所周知的【大衛城】。此後，國家逐漸替代支派，支派的權力逐漸消逝、去而不返。

由於政治和軍事的成功，以色列在大衛的管治下成為一個統一的王國，但是分裂的種子因王位承繼的問題早已種植下來，妒忌與憎恨發生於眾子之間。最終，所羅門在宮廷斗爭中脫穎而出，奪得王權，以卑劣的手段鏟除異己手足，鞏固實力。

所羅門經濟繁重的背後，是國家權力集中，苛捐雜稅繁重的高昂代價。訴諸於強迫勞役，甚至不惜使用奴隸......這是神的意願嗎？

所羅門時代社會結構最大的變遷，是國家權力替代了支派聯盟及其宗教和神治的權力。上帝所設立的12個支派維系民族的計劃被歪曲，12支派的獨立不復存在，社會基本的責任不再是與神的盟約，國家權力取而代之。

北國以色列拒絕接受大衛家族做他們永遠的王，抗拒改朝換代及所羅門的暴虐獨裁，南北雙方張力日增。

因此，所羅門死後，國家分裂並不意外。所羅門的兒子羅波安在處理北方各族的問題上的自大和愚妄，更加劇了國家的頹勢與分裂。民族迅即不再強大，南北雙方國勢減弱，惡王當道，謀殺繼位之事層出不窮，亞述和巴比倫更是將王國推入尾聲。

選民悖逆神，以一己的方法取代與神的盟約，令國家衰退腐爛。對於我們來說，最大的功課就是，即使最智慧的王，若不能與神同行，謹守主旨，仍不算智慧。

詩篇說："你們不要依靠君王，不要依靠世人，他一點不能幫助，他的氣一斷就歸回塵土，他所打算的當日就消滅了，以雅各的神為幫助"（詩146:3-5）

The Cross

The Cross ranks among the most mysterious of mysteries in Christianity. The mystery of the Cross is the dark center of Christian light, the spring of its central meaning. We never stop struggling to try to comprehend its horror, absurdity, and inescapable necessity. We live and die by the Cross, but do we really understand it?

Horror, because an innocent man was hung on the cross for many hours before dying. Absurdity, because mortal men killed their God. Necessity, because only this sinless sacrificial lamb can nullify the sins of humanity.

Each of us, at different times, is crucifier and crucified. We are part of the crowd that called for Christ's execution, and we are crucified by our sins. How can we escape our complicity in the death of Christ when we shouted, "Give us Barabbas", whoever Barabbas was. Who cares who he was? We would take him anyway. Let him go and crucify Christ.

What was His guilt? Perhaps, a less execrable pretext could have been fabricated. Blasphemy would do. But the fact was, make what you will, He lay stigmatized, a broken and humiliated God the world had sport of. We even offered Him vinegar for His thirst.

Stepping beyond the mystery of the Cross, we tried to bury Christ crucified, the only begotten Son, sacrificed to human flesh and finite time and all our sin. Unless we grieve like Mary at His grave, giving Him up as lost, no Easter morning comes.

十字架

基督教的十字架乃神秘中的神秘。它是基督教眾光之中最隱晦難明的部分，卻是基督教信仰的源頭。我們從未曾停止過一種努力---努力去解讀它的望而生畏、它的荒謬絕倫，它的必不可少。或生或死，我們的生命都基於十字架，但又有多少人真正了解其內涵呢？

望而生畏，實在是因為一個無辜的人被挂在木頭上幾個小時而漸漸痛苦地死去；

荒謬絕倫，實在是因為凡人竟然殺了自己的神；

必不可少，卻又是因為唯有這無瑕無疵的羔羊才能洗淨世人的罪。

在不同的時刻，我們每個人都可能是釘人者，同時也是被釘者。我們既是人群中喊著釘耶穌十字架的一個，我們也是因罪被釘死的一個。基督受難的日子，有誰能脫罪呢？當我們高喊“釋放巴拉巴”的時候，我們甚至不曉得此為何許人也，做過些什麼。不過，有誰在乎他呢？我們寧願放過巴拉巴，也不能放過耶穌！那麼，耶穌究竟何罪之有呢？或者人祗是為了找個不那麼差勁的借口來釘死祂罷了！那麼祂自以為神以至於褻瀆，就是義正詞嚴的理由了。但事實上，無論人們如何尋找藉口，世人確實用羞辱、破碎和玩弄讓他們的上帝死去，甚至用醋為臨終的祂解渴。

徘徊於這神秘的十字架前，我們試圖將被釘的基督埋葬了；不料這位上帝獨生的子卻是為著我們這些酒囊飯袋且惡貫滿盈的人死了。除非我們如同馬利亞一般，在祂的墓前，因著失去祂而悲傷懊悔，否則復活的晨光將永遠不會臨到。

The Inn of the Sixth Happiness: Gladys Aylward I

In 1957, the book, "The Small Woman", was published and became a major film, "*The Inn of the Sixth Happiness*", starring Ingrid Bergman. An irate viewer wrote to Newsweek magazine, "In order for a movie to be good, the story should be believable!" Such was the life of Gladys Aylward who heard God's call in an evangelistic meeting to be a missionary for China in 1930. She was penniless in London and lacked the education to qualify for missionary support. She placed her almost empty purse on top of her bible and cried out, "Oh, God, here's my bible! Here is my money! Use me, God!". Voyage to China by boat was far too costly but she managed to scrape together the fare for the Trans-Siberian Railway, working as a house-maid and trained herself as an evangelist by mounting a soap box in Hyde Park to preach. God answered her with a call from a lone missionary in China's remote Shanxi province.

The journey through Siberia almost ended her life through savagery of nature and humanity. She eventually met up with Mrs. Lawson at Yangcheng by muleback. To survive, the two missionary women decided to spruce up their ramshackle house for the muleteers of the caravans passing through this town, as a hostel, for man and beast. With a large measure of optimism, they chose the name "Inn of Eight Happinesses", after the Chinese probity of Love, Virtue, Gentleness, Tolerance, Loyalty, Truth, Beauty, and Devotion. For unknown reasons, Hollywood perverted the name to "Inn of the Sixth Happiness".

Gladys, barely five feet tall, the small woman, learned quickly to aim for the lead mule of a caravan and drag the animal into the inn's courtyard by its bridle. Once done, the battle was won. No way would the mules leave the promise of food and rest. The ulterior motive of housing the mule teams was the chance to share the gospels with the muleteers, as free entertainment, or story time. Gladys was becoming native, but the shock of Mrs. Lawson's sudden accidental death punctured the calm of her life. She was alone. God came to her rescue with a new ministry.

China banned the practice of foot-binding of women. The local mandarin decided Gladys would make a perfect enforcer of this new law. She was a woman with big feet. She could enter houses with impunity, as official "foot inspector". The whole province was now open to her evangelism. Families welcomed her. In the evenings, villagers crowded around her to listen to the stories she told of a man called Jesus Christ, whose honorable ancestor was the great God who lived in the heaven above. The people understood that this man Jesus had lived in a simple society like theirs. He was an enthralling person, and the foot inspector's supply of captivating stories seemed inexhaustible.

It would have been a heart-warming and soul-satisfying story if Gladys was destined to glorify God in this lasting manner. I hope the subsequent events in her life will be interesting to you. We thank God for the role model of this small woman. The story of Gladys up to this point is reminiscent of 1Corinthians 1:26-27, "Brothers, think of what you were by human standards; not many were influential; not many were of noble birth. But God chose the foolish things of the world to shame the wise; God chose the weak things of the world to shame the strong."

六福棧 一

1953年【小婦人】一書出版后，被改變為一部由英國女星英格麗褒曼主演的著名電影，名曰『六福棧』。有個觀眾看後十分反感，致信反映說，一部好的電影，故事當有較高的可信度，但是這個故事並不可信。

今天我會提到艾德韋這個人，她的故事就更加難以置信......

上個世紀30年代，艾德韋在倫敦聽聞神要她去中國傳道的呼召。當時的她既身無分文，也不夠條件申請傳道經費。於是，她將空錢包放在聖經上面禱告說：神啊，這是我的聖經，這是我的錢包，請你使用我吧！當時，由倫敦到中國的旅費十分昂貴，而她所存的錢，僅僅夠由倫敦經西伯利亞到中國的火車票。為了這次旅行，她多方預備自己，她曾為人打掃清潔，甚至將箱子放在公園裡，訓練自己站在上面向路人講道。神應允 她的禱告。很快她收到邀請，前往中國山西去幫助一個孤寡老太。

途徑西伯利亞的旅程兵荒馬亂，險象環生，騎在驢上的她險些喪命。經過數月奔波，終於在陽城見到這位太太。但是分文全無的兩個女人如何過活？她們想盡辦法將所居住的房子重新油漆，修繕妥當，成為騎驢過客的棲身之所。她們樂觀的為這個房子起名叫做【八福棧】。（不知何故，荷裡活後來將之改為【六福棧】。）

艾德韋身材瘦小，卻曉得如何招攬生意，靈活地將過路客頭匹驢的韁繩拉到手。她招攬過客留宿最大的目的，是向驢夫傳講福音，而這些疲乏的宿客也很樂意聆聽免費的福音故事。艾德韋很快適應了中國的生活，但不幸的是她的女伴意外跌死，祇剩下艾德韋孤身一人。

1930年，中國法律禁止女人扎腳，陽城官員啟用艾德韋，讓她巡視檢查女人扎腳的狀況，她行走自如的履行職責，隨時以女士身份進入不同的家庭中，可謂名副其實的女腳檢查官。

羊城四處都她的足跡，艾德韋的名字受到很多家庭的歡迎。在不同的家庭裡，她向人述說福音，告訴人們耶穌基督的故事，讓他們知道，上帝是住在雲端上最偉大的神，耶穌曾經來到世界，住在人群當中。深諳故事技巧的她吸引了大量的聽眾，她的傳道方法溫暖人心，令無數個靈魂得到滿足。

上帝使用這個小女人，讓她成為今天我們傳道的榜樣，回應了哥林多前書的話："弟兄們啊，可見你們蒙召，按肉體，有智慧的不多，有能力的不多，有尊貴的也不多。神卻揀選了世上愚拙的，叫有智慧的羞愧。揀選了世上軟弱的，叫那強壯的羞愧。"（林前1:26-27）

The Inn of the Sixth Happiness: Gladys Aylward II

As if being the official foot inspector was not enough, a most unusual duty was presented to Gladys, for which she dared not fail. A mad man was wielding a chopper in the local prison. Blood was everywhere. No one was brave enough to enter it. The head of the prison implored Gladys to help. "Why me? I am just a missionary woman. I will be killed." The rejoinder was, "How can they kill you? You claim that you have the living God inside you." Gladys thought to herself, "Fail now and I am finished in Yangcheng. Abandon my faith now, and I abandon it forever!" She went inside. The mad man chased another inmate who ran in her direction. Numb with fear, she confronted him and said, "Give me that chopper!" For what seemed like hours, he glared at her. Then suddenly he meekly handed over the chopper. She could only feel sadness and pity for all the miserable remnants of humanity in that prison. "I will ask the prison head to deal leniently with you, and I will be back to help you." One prisoner came up to her and said, "Thank you, Ai-weh-deh." Later she learned that this meant "The Virtuous One". She was known by that name ever since.

She began to acquire a “family” adopting foundling. The first child was bought for nine pence and she named her Ninepence. She felt so tied to China, she became a Chinese citizen in 1936.

The Japanese war machine did not spare Yangcheng. Bombs fell and Gladys worked tirelessly with the Mandarin to nurse the wounded. After the Japanese soldiers passed through the deserted town, she and the people returned from the hills. Her inn was damaged and the trade would diminish in war. The Mandarin held a dinner, perhaps the last feast in Yangcheng for a very long time to come as the war dragged on. At the end of the dinner, the Mandarin stood up to tell everyone how Ai-deh-weh had come to Yangcheng and what she had done for the poor and the sick and the imprisoned. He confided that he had discussed and studied the faith which she brought with her in private on many occasions. He turned to her and said, "I would like, Ai-deh-weh, to embrace your faith. I would like to become a Christian."

六福棧 二

身為女腳檢查官的人，無論在當時，還是今日都可以說是微乎其微。除此之外，艾德韋還遇到一樁難以推卸的事件。

有一日，官方請艾德韋去監獄見一個人。眼前的一幕令人難以置信---一個人正揮舞菜刀在監獄裡瘋狂地殺人，鮮血遍地，見者膽寒，巡視的哨兵、警察皆無勇氣靠近現場，監獄長唯有請艾德韋前來調停制止。她說："為什麼是我呢？我是一個小女人，祇是來傳道，去見他，我會被殺死的。"監獄長說："此人不敢殺你，因為你的身上有位活神，沒有人能夠殺死你。"艾德韋心想：如果我不能成功的制止他，在陽城我將無所作為。我若放棄我的信心，我將會永遠放棄了。於是，她存著信心，向那個正在追斬人的狂者走去。被殺之人見到她，就向她跑來，如此場面令她倍感驚慌。面對面遭遇狂者，她祇簡單地說了一句話----"將刀給我！"眾目睽睽之下，狂者出人意外地將刀交在她的手裡。心懷同情的她，對所有獄囚說，她會向監獄長求情，赦免他們。當中一個囚犯向她鞠躬行禮，緩緩道出："你一定就是艾德韋！"

艾德韋，一個滿有美德的名字，從此之後，她正式啟用這個名字。

後來的年月，艾德韋組織了一個收養孤兒的家庭，其中一個孩子是用九個便士買來的，於是她便稱呼這個孩子"九便士"。

她深感自己就是中國之一分子，直至1936年，正式成為中國公民。適逢日本侵略中國，戰爭機器不會放過陽城，炸彈轟鳴之中，她穿梭於傷者之間，奮力救死扶傷。日軍入城，人們四處疏散，舉城空曠，待日軍撤走，呈現的盡是滿目瘡痍、廢墟滿地。陽城市長舉辦最後一個、也是多日未有的晚餐會。艾 德韋被邀前往，晚宴終了，市長起身演講，特別提及這位仁慈的女士，她如何來到這個城市、如何幫助顧惜市民、窮人、甚至囚犯....最終，市長言及艾德韋所傳的耶穌基督，說，"艾德韋，我想信教，做基督徒！"

The Inn of the Sixth Happiness: Gladys Aylward III

In 1940, Gladys traveled to a neighboring city under Japanese occupation to help a missionary couple. Her efforts to stop an attempted rape at this mission by some rogue soldiers rewarded her with painful internal injuries which she carried for the rest of her life. She also inherited 200 children from that mission who had to be evacuated to the safety of Chungking, the war time capital of China, but first they had to reach Sian. A guide had delivered a first group of children but he did not return for the 100 remaining. He was probably captured by the Japanese. Gladys had no choice but to try to walk the children herself over mountains and wilderness, especially after learning that she was on the wanted list of the occupation army. It was almost too late. She was hit by a bullet, but she survived. The Christian Mandarin asked how she would cross the dangerous territory with no money and no food. Her reply, "God will provide." "Yes," he answered, "but on this occasion, at least, let the Mandarin of Yangcheng act as His agent. I can provide you with two baskets of millet and two men to carry them for the first part of your journey. It will take you weeks to reach Sian." They bowed low to each other. The hardship of the journey was brutal. When they came to the Yellow River, there was no way to cross it. One woman and 100 children, tired, hungry and shoeless. "Ai-deh-weh, why does not God open the waters of the Yellow River for us to cross as He did for the Israelites?" She did not know how to tell a hurt and hungry child that miracles were not just for the asking. Out of desperation, she asked the children to gather around to sing a hymn to God. The strange sounds reached the ears of a scouting platoon of the Chinese soldiers lying in wait for the Japanese. They helped the tottering group to cross. Still steep mountains stood in their way. Exhaustion forced many rests. On one of these, Gladys felt something wet flowing down her cheeks. She was sobbing uncontrollably from sheer weakness and exhaustion, for all the children, for all China, and for all the world. The tears cleansed her soul, washed away the bleak desperation. She did not remember how many days the trip lasted, probably over a month. They staggered into a refugee camp outside Sian, just in time because she fell into a delirium and had to be delivered to a Scandinavian mission in an oxcart. Eventually she recovered to some degree from her multiple wounds and diseases but blackouts and spells of mental derangement continued to torture her. She eventually went back to England but returned to Taiwan where she died.

Buried among her heroic and unbelievable acts of mercy, she gave priority to God's work in denying herself a love relationship that developed between her and a Chinese military officer. Their courtship had to be sacrificed, with so much work to be done in the Lord's name for the people of

China. The war parted them and through all the rest of her waking days, she would remember the one man she had loved. Although Gladys was not able to find him, she found God's everlasting love.

We are touched by so many lessons in her life, we would not be human if we did not share her tears.

六福棧 三

1940年日戰期間，艾德韋赴另一日軍佔領的城市去幫助一對宣教夫婦，嘗試制止日軍暴力，卻不幸被日軍打至嚴重內傷，留下難以愈合的傷痛。

此次行程，她接收了被遣往重慶的200個小童。前往重慶必須經過西安，一位向導疑被日軍俘虜，在護送100位小童抵達西安的路上失去蹤跡。故此，艾德韋祗能帶另外的100位小童，經荒野山嶺徒步向重慶進發。日軍四處通緝她，子彈又意外地射傷了她，幾乎不能成行，但到底保住了性命。成為基督徒的市長問她："沒有錢晌、沒有口糧，如何成行？"她堅定地說："神會供應。"市長雖點頭稱是，但慮及路程遙遠，願助一臂之力，即派手下助艾德韋背若干路程的糧食。艾德韋向市長深深鞠躬告別。路途艱辛、一個小女子要照顧百多小童、勞累、 飢餓、鞋子都沒有了。面對難以逾越的黃河，眾孩童詢問說："你說上帝帶領以色列人過紅海，為什麼今天上帝不能帶我們過河？"艾德韋無言以對，唯默默地說："神跡非人力能夠擺布。"絕望加上勞累，她將所有的孩童招聚身邊，請大家一同唱一首聖詩。歌聲傳至埋伏於四周的中國兵士的耳中，他們前來相助，護送這群婦孺過河。然而，河的那邊仍然矗立著險峻的山嶺……大家走走停停，淚水在艾德韋的臉上不可抑制的淌留，為了孩子，為了中國，為了世界，她的眼淚止不住的流出，以致不再記得哭泣之後如何攜帶眾孩童繼續上路。

此次旅行，整整逾時個把月，終於抵達西安附近的難民營。跨越門欄的一刻，艾德韋就暈倒了。一位傳道人套牛車將她送到北歐的傳道驛站接受治療。旅途的艱險、身體的消耗、傷口雖得以治愈，但難以抹去心靈的傷痛。偶然間，艾德韋的情緒會變得不可抑制的失控。後來，她返回英國接受治療。回中國時輾轉前往台灣，後逝於台灣。

在滿有憐憫的一生中，艾德韋始終將上帝置於生命的首位，因使命在身，她擱置了與一位中國軍人的愛情，戰爭分離了她和她的愛人，直死未能相見。她的故事深深觸動人心，聽者無不一掬同情淚水。但在上帝那裡，艾德韋必會找到更美麗、更深情的愛，非地上之愛能夠比擬。

服侍上帝傳教士的生命，似乎不可避免地與艱苦、犧牲劃上等號。他們要克服常人難以逾越之高山、荒野與河流；要付上生命之代價，甚至被葬於異鄉的黃土。其故事鮮人知曉，但上帝在祂的國度裡，為他們存留著永不朽壞的榮耀冠冕。為著這個冠冕，讓我們學效先聖，追其佳美腳蹤。

Protestantism and Reformation

When we think of the Protestant movement, we tend to visualize Martin Luther nailing the ninety five theses on the door of the Castle Church in Wittenberg in 1517. That was the start of the Reformation in Germany. Luther did not plan to separate from the Catholic Church. He sought to correct the errors of the doctrines while conserving the rest, within the church. He was very concerned about his own salvation. His excommunication sealed the fate of any reconciliation. The Lutheran church was born. It did not take long for another church, the Reformed church to arrive.

Ulrich Zwingli, a Catholic priest in Zurich, Switzerland, was also unhappy with the church. He was a more radical reformer. Zwingli and Luther shared many similar thoughts but also had outstanding disagreements. They met in 1529 in a debate known as the Colloquy of Marburg. Their differences remained. This is the source of the Reformed church, a reformation within the Protestant movement. It is a more radical separation from the Catholic doctrines. Later, John Calvin succeeded Zwingli in establishing the Reformed church. John Knox brought it to Scotland. In a sense, this was the origin of the long story of denominational development in Protestantism.

To illustrate such differences, we can look at the divergence of doctrine regarding the last supper or Holy Communion. The confessional Lutherans believe in transubstantiation of the bread and wine into the body and blood of Christ. When the Lutheran communicant receives the consecrated bread and wine, he is not merely partaking in a meal of remembrance. Christ unites with him physically. On the other hand, Presbyterians believe that Christ is spiritually present in the bread and wine. These different beliefs arise from different interpretations of the same scripture, Luke 22:19-20, "And he took bread, gave thanks and broke it, and gave it to them, saying, 'This is my body given for you; do this in remembrance of me.' In the same way, after the supper he took the cup saying,' this cup is the new covenant in my blood, which is poured out for you."

There are literally hundreds of Protestant denominations today differing in doctrines, traditions, and liturgical rites. They, however, share in one important outlook, the liberty of conscience, which has led to diversity of belief and practice.

It is amazing that an underlying unity still permeates the vast diversity in Protestant thoughts. The immutable scripture and salvation by faith are the constants.

新教與改革運動

每逢提及新教運動，1517年馬丁•路德將95條論綱釘在維滕貝格城堡教堂門上的一幕便會油然而生。路德在糾正教義謬誤的同時，力圖保留其余教義，并無意將自己由天主教會中分離開來，卻是十分重視個人的得救。此乃德國改教的起始。被逐出教會後，被凍結與無從和解的命運，令路德感到此乃既成事實，無可更改。隨後，路德宗誕生，另一個歸正教會亦應運而生。

烏爾裡希•慈溫理，一位瑞士蘇黎世的天主教神甫，同樣是個激進且對教會不滿的改革者。在眾多方面茨溫理和路德觀點類似，但雙方也存在着明顯的分歧。1529年，兩人於馬爾堡討論會的辯論上相遇，分歧依然存在，導致了一個較離開天主教更為激進的分離，即路德會由新教運動內部的改革中，與歸正教會分道揚鑣。後來，約翰•加爾文繼慈溫理衣缽，成為歸正宗的領袖，而約翰•諾克斯則將它帶到蘇格蘭。由某種意義上說，此乃新教漫長歷史的起源。

後來，透過有關聖餐的教義，雙方的差異得到了較為貼切的闡述與表達。

路德宗相信聖餐變質說。聖餐中的餅和杯，一經祝聖即成為基督的身體和血。路德宗的聖餐禮，紀念的不僅是一餐飯，更是與基督身體的合一。另一方面，長老會相信，存在於餅與杯中的，是基督靈性層面的臨在。此種差異源於不同教派對路加福音22:19-20的不同解釋：“他拿起餅來，祝謝了，就擘開，遞給了他們，說：這是我的身體，為你們舍的，你們每逢吃的時候，要如此行，為的是紀念我。飯后，照樣拿杯來說，這杯是我的血所立的新約，為你們流出。”

今天，數以百計的新教教派，擁有各自不同的教義、傳統和崇拜禮儀。然而，在分享信仰共同遠景的同時，自由和良心，豐富著信仰及其實踐，使之更為多元、更為多姿多彩。奇妙的是，雖然新教思想博大多元，但潛在的一致是基於不變的經文，及因信得救的信仰。

The Roots of Presbyterianism

We all know that Christianity spread throughout the Roman Empire both in the West (Latin influence) and in the East (Greek influence). The Western development centered around Rome whose Bishop claimed primacy among his peers. This led to the Roman Catholic Church and the Papacy. For many centuries, this Roman Church was the church in western civilization, despite many internal problems of heresies and political divisions.

By the early 14th century, nationalism, opposition to the oppressive fund raising by the church, the Renaissance of rationalistic philosophy, and the moral laxity among many clergy, began to foment a populist movement against the church establishment. The splits within the papacy itself did nothing to help. At one time, there were three popes all claiming to be the head of the church, each excommunicating the other two. Many years passed before a single pope was finally installed again in Rome in the year 1417. You would think that the church would have learned a lesson and would make amends. On the contrary, the papacy became extravagant, almost pagan in its quest for luxury with insatiable appetites for money to build grand cathedrals. This gave rise to the famous doctrine of indulgences which in the end stages meant that money could buy absolution of guilt before God, without confession or contrition.

Although Martin Luther stood out as the icon of the Reformation, there were some other very dedicated reformers who preceded him in many parts of Europe. In the words of one historian, Europe was "a seething kettle by year 1500, ready to boil over." Luther provided a channel for this outburst. He emphasized the priesthood of the believer and his right to go directly to God and to interpret the Scripture for himself. On Oct.31, 1517, Luther posted his famous "Ninety-Five Theses" on the church door in protest. He was fortunate to find protection with a German Lord, short of which he would have been burnt at the stakes. His movement became known as the Protestant or Lutheran movement. He preached three core beliefs: 1) Justification by faith alone; 2) Salvation by Grace alone; 3) Bible, the only source of authority.

Among the reformers, there emerged differing theological concepts, not surprisingly. One of these thinkers was John Calvin who was French but worked in Switzerland. He published his famous "Institutes of the Christian Religion" at the age of twenty six and rose to be the leading voice of the Reformation in all but the Lutheran lands.

Probably in no country in Europe had the Reformation arrived in better timing than in Scotland, where the Roman Catholic clergy had sunk into the deepest morass. The physical separation between Scotland and the major centers of Christianity had something to do with this. Reformers were martyred by the depraved clergy. One of these martyrs was a follower of John Calvin. His legacy was entrusted to John Knox who led the Scottish movement which culminated in the recognition of the Church of Scotland by Parliament in 1560 and the proclamation of the First Scottish Confession along the lines of Calvinism.

Later, when Scotland united with England into Great Britain, the Church of Scotland maintained her independence from the Church of England. Presbyterianism became synonymous with the Church of Scotland. The distinguishing characteristics are its democratic polity and its communal theology in Confessions. The Presbyterian Church, (U.S.A.), is a natural outgrowth as British peoples immigrated to America.

溯本追源長老宗

我們知道基督教曾遍傳包括受希臘及拉丁文化影響的東西羅馬帝國。西方的發展以羅馬為中心。主教為首，導致了羅馬大公教會及教皇制度。許多世紀以來，即使異端、內部紛爭與政治分野層出不窮，羅馬教會依然是西方文明中唯一幸存的教會。

14世紀初葉，國家主義、教會集資的壓力、文藝復興的理性哲學、聖品人員的道德鬆弛、民粹主義運動，都抗衡著羅馬教會的建制。教皇制度內部的分裂令矛盾加劇。曾於同一時間，三個教皇互相排擠，同時宣稱自己是教會的頭。就此歷時多年，直1417年，羅馬教皇才最終任命了唯一的主教。教會本當因此有所醒悟，可惜事與願違。教皇越發奢侈放肆，因興建富麗堂皇的大教堂變得貪婪無度，最終引致贖罪的教義，即在神面前，以購買贖罪券，來代替悔改與認罪。

在馬丁路德挺身而出，成為改教的代言人之前，歐洲已出現過許多獻身改教之人。套用一位歷史學家的話，歐洲彷佛"一壺沸騰了1500年的水，隨時滾過沸點，溢出壺外。"而路德不過為這個沸騰提供了一個渠道。他強調信徒皆祭司，人人皆可直接到神那裡、人人皆可直接領受聖經。1517年10月31日，路德據理力爭，於教會門上貼出他著名的【95條論綱】，並有幸受到一名德國皇嗣的保護，使他免受火刑。他所推動的這個運動即是現在廣為人知的新教或路德宗。路德的論點主要有三："唯獨信心，唯獨恩典，唯獨聖經"。

當時，不同的神學理念紛紛出籠。眾多改教者中，生於法國、工作於瑞士的神學家、思想家約翰•加爾文於26歲那年頒布了其举世闻名的【基督教教義】，其強烈的呼聲，使改教運動超越本土，影響了世界。

當時，或者沒有一個國家能像蘇格蘭那樣更具改革的契機。羅馬聖品人員的頹敗，令新教的主流思想於蘇格蘭的傳播成為可能。當然改革亦遭受極度迫害，改教運動中殉道的有約翰 • 加爾文的追隨者。而約翰•諾克斯作為其思想遺產的承繼者，曾繼續帶領蘇格蘭的改革，並於1560年將改教推至巔峰。

蘇格蘭教會最終得到國家議會認可，發布了師從加爾文路線的蘇格蘭教會信仰告白書。後來，蘇格蘭與英國合並為大不列顛，長老宗與蘇格蘭教會亦融為一體，祇是仍然保留各自的民主政體與共有的神學告白。當英國人移居美洲之後，隨之設立的美國長老會自然成為英國長老宗的一個分支。

A Layman's View of Christianity vs. Islam

All of us are familiar with the story of Abraham in Genesis. He was childless until at the suggestion of his first wife, he married his second wife, Hagar, who bore him Ishmael. His first wife, Sarah, also became the mother of another son, Isaac, 13 years later. Jews and Christians believe that Isaac was the rightful heir of Abraham while Muslims claim Ishmael as their patriarch. This split in the family tree of Abraham is the simplistic root of the centuries-old feud in the Middle East.

From our vantage point, let us try to discover how the major features of Islam, the faith of Muslims, differ from Christianity. Islam means submission to Allah or God who has sent many prophets notably including Abraham, Moses, and Jesus. According to Islam, His final and greatest prophet was Muhammad in year 610 A.D. Muslims believe God is One, not the Holy Trinity of Father, Son, and the Holy Spirit. They consider the bible corrupted in the hands of Christians and believe that the angel Gabriel revealed the real truth to Mohammad who left these words to his followers who collected them in the Quran, the sacred book of Islam. The Quran is considered divine only in its original Arabic form and Muslims study and recite it only in Arabic, regardless of the person's ethnicity or native language. Perhaps, a great salient contrast between Islam and Christianity lies in the differing ultimate attribute of God: Will for the Muslims and Love for the Christians. Another point of divergence is that the great reward for a Muslim is an eternal paradise of pleasures while Christians look to enjoy God's fulfilling presence in eternity.

Islam rejects the idea that God had a divine Son whose blood redeemed mankind. Crucifixion was a hoax. The Quran contradicts the bible in many places.

Muslims believe good deeds weigh against bad deeds while Christians believe in grace through faith, good works not sufficing.

Even though the same God, the God of Abraham, is worshipped by Muslims and by Christians, in practice, the two religions differ significantly. The most fundamental difference is this: Christianity claims Jesus to be the Son of God; Islam identifies Him as merely a prophet. It is an insurmountable fundamental barrier.

Another looming issue comes from the militant factions of Muslims. It concerns the doctrine of abrogation or annulment. It teaches that later revelations in the Quran have superseded earlier ones. Earlier peaceful verses have been cancelled and annulled-they are no longer valid. Newer and more violent verses have taken their place. This has added to the tension between Muslims and non-Muslims. The radicals follow this doctrine. It is hoped that in time the moderates can affirm the original peaceful verses and we can all live in peace.

(References for this article can be found in the "Decision" magazine, a Billy Graham publication, September 2010)

基督教與回教的異同

亞伯拉罕在創世紀中的故事眾所周知。他原本沒有兒女，直到侍女夏甲生以實瑪利，13年後妻子撒拉生以撒。猶太人和基督徒相信以撒是亞伯拉罕的後裔，但回教徒則認為以實瑪利才是嫡系。在亞伯拉罕的族譜中，兩個原本簡單的分岔，卻在中東歷史上引發了漫長的爭拗。

我們需要留意伊斯蘭教和基督教的異同。伊斯蘭教徒降服於阿拉的旨意。認為阿拉曾經差遣過很多的先知，亞伯拉罕，摩西、耶穌等都是其中的先知，但最后一位先知，是公元后610年阿拉所差遣的穆罕默德。

與基督教的三一神論迥異的是，伊斯蘭教徒篤信一神論，否認聖父聖子與聖靈。認為聖經已被基督徒篡改，唯一的啟示，是經由天使加百列報告給穆罕默德，穆罕默德傳授與弟子，以阿拉伯文書寫，經門徒整理取名的【可蘭經】。不分種族語言，所有回教徒都以阿拉伯文誦讀【可蘭經】。但【可蘭經】與【聖經】沖突頗多。

在有關神屬性的問題上，回教徒認為神是意志，但基督徒認為神是愛。

回教徒認為死後的天堂是一個享樂的所在，但基督徒認為天堂是一個與神永遠同在的地方。

回教徒不信上帝獨生子流血的救贖，認為釘十字架是場鬧劇。以不同的途徑反駁聖經。認為好行為能夠抵銷罪；但是基督徒認為，人靠自己不能脫罪，需要依靠神的恩典、聖子及祂寶血的救贖。

基督教與回教都敬拜亞伯拉罕的神，但雙方有無法逾越的障礙，主要區別是，回教徒認為耶穌衹不過是個先知，基督徒則認為耶穌是神的聖子。

今天，新一代回教極端分子崇尚武力，舊式和平版本的【可蘭經】 頗有可能被充滿暴力的新版所取代，更加加深了回教徒與非回教徒間的張力，令兩下二分為一。

切望回教溫和派能夠重新肯定原有和平的舊版【可蘭經】，令世界和睦相處。

（此文參考2010年9月葛培禮所出版的Decision雜志）

What Sacraments Are

A sacrament is an outward sign instituted by God in which God has joined His Word of promise to the visible elements by which He offers, gives, and seals the forgiveness of sin, earned by Christ. An alternate statement is that a sacrament is an efficacious sign of grace by Christ, whereby divine life is dispensed to us, embodied in an outward sign of an inward and spiritual grace ordained by Christ so that we receive the same and a pledge of assurance.

How many sacraments are there? The Presbyterian Church believes in two sacraments, Baptism and the Lord's Supper or Holy Communion. Baptism washes away our sins. Like the resurrected Christ, we are born anew, dead to sin but alive to God (Roman 6:11). It symbolizes a change in a person's eternal destiny. Holy Communion was begun by Jesus, Himself, on the night He was betrayed. Giving wine and bread to His disciples, He said, "This is my body and this is my blood." The disciples did not really understand those words at the time. (Luke 22:14-23). Later, the true meaning became known: Jesus was the Ultimate Sacrifice for our sin, to bring redemption.

The Roman Catholic Church decided around the year 1200 AD that there were seven sacraments while later Protestant Churches stayed with two.

The ancient meaning of sacrament had a ring of mystery to it, implying the hidden plan of God to save mankind through Jesus Christ. Paul mentioned this hidden plan (Rom 16:25, Eph. 3:3).

The Catholic Church notably believes in the transubstantiation of the Elements, whereby the elements change into the body and blood of Christ. Most Protestant churches believe in the symbolic nature.

Baptism is carried out differently in different churches-immersion or sprinkling.

何謂聖禮

聖禮, 如同一個外在的標志，由上帝設立, 將其承諾的話語融入可見的聖餐，透過耶穌基督頒賜予人，使罪得赦。另一種說法是，聖禮乃基督恩典可見的表象，將屬神的生命頒賜與人。聖禮由基督所立、是內在屬靈恩典外在的體現，為使我們得著有效的保障與承諾。

聖禮有多少種呢？長老宗認為有兩種聖禮，即洗禮和聖餐禮。

洗禮，代表罪被洗滌淨盡，如同復活的主，洗禮後成為重生的人，向罪死、向上帝活（羅6:11），象征著人生命的改變。

聖餐禮，則由基督於被賣的那一夜親自設立，他將餅和杯遞給門徒說，“這是我的身體……這是我立約的血”。當時, 門徒並不真正理解這番話語的含義 (路22:14-23)。其後，聖餐的意義廣為人知：因着人的罪, 耶穌基督成為永遠的祭，祂將救贖賜給我們。

公元后1200年羅馬天主教決定了七種聖禮，後來的新教教會祗採納其中的兩種。

在遠古的意識裡，人們認為有一個神秘的環在聖禮當中，意味著上帝隱藏的、透過耶穌基督拯救人類的計劃。保羅曾經在羅馬書與以弗所書中提及此隱藏的計劃（羅16:25；弗3:3）。

天主教會尤其相信，聖餐中“餅”成為基督的身體，“杯”成為基督寶血的變質說；而新教教會則傾向於聖餐的象征意義。

洗禮在不同的教會中，表達的形式不甚一致，有的教會傾向點水禮，有的則注重浸水禮。

THE BETTER FOLLOWERS OF JESUS

作主門徒

Do You Hear His Call?

Christ's call is "Follow me." It means to go after, to submit to the will of the one who leads. It draws out personal obedience, loyalty, and fidelity. It suggests a soldier's allegiance for his commander. A follower places himself in the service of the person he seeks to follow. The martyred German disciple, Dietrich Bonhoeffer, said, "When we are called to follow Christ, we are summoned to an exclusive attachment to His person." To follow Christ is to take the first step of discipleship.

The call is an open invitation to all men, not merely a chosen few, but only the chosen respond in acceptance. We must be careful not to confuse our readiness to follow with our own degree of goodness or piety or understanding. The call can surprise us anywhere and anytime whether we are ready or not. Our state of holiness is not relevant. Even the disciples did not know much about Jesus when He called to them.

They had no qualifications. "Follow me and I will make you become fishers of men. / And immediately they left their nets and followed Him." (Mark 1:17-18). The call demands a response. There are only two responses. Renounce it or risk all for it. To become disciples and witnesses involves a decision to risk everything for Christ.

In today's business climate we are used to study and analyze a proposition in a number of ways before we would come near a decision. In reacting to Jesus' call, we are tempted to try to adapt what Jesus is saying to our more comfortable life style. We want to explain away or water down what Jesus is calling us to do. The plain fact is, "If any man would come after me, let him deny himself and take up his cross and follow me." Jesus did not say, "Would you like to try my philosophical system or code of ethics?" He is not approaching us as a salesman or even a moralist. He is in our face, as the Son of God. There is no compromise. There is no discussion or negotiation. We are to follow Him on His terms, not ours. Jesus knows the cost of following Him. That's why He does not make a call lightly. See Luke 9:57-62, where He turned down three prospects.

A legitimate question is, "What is in it for me to follow Him?" Peter even asked this. (Matt. 10:27). "What then shall we have?" Eternal life is the answer which is only meaningful to those whom God has chosen. In today's commercial reality, we are tempted to postpone our moment of decision until we know all the intellectual answers or data or until we find higher probabilities of reward. Answers can only come when we walk with faith on the path of pilgrimage.

聽聞呼召？

基督的呼召是“跟隨我”！意味著要追隨、服從一位帶領者的意志。“跟隨我”強調的是個人的服從、忠心和真誠，如同軍人效忠他的將領。一位跟隨者願意將自己交托在一位值得跟隨的人手上。德國殉道士潘霍華說，“當我們被呼召跟隨耶穌，我們乃是被召和耶穌成為一體。”跟隨耶穌，是做門徒的第一步。

基督呼召、邀請的對象是所有人，並非是少數人，但是唯有選民會接受。需要留意的是，無論一個人處於何種程度，多麼良善、敬虔和理解，任何地點、任何時間耶穌的呼召都可能臨到他。即使耶穌的門徒，當他們被召的時候，並不是很深入地認識耶穌基督。

這些門徒資格不夠、學識短少。但當他們聽見耶穌說，“跟隨我，我要使你們得人如得魚”的時候，他們立時放棄維生的漁網，起身跟隨（可1：17-18）。神的呼召需要人的回應。回應有兩種：或是漠視呼召、或者不計代價立時跟隨。作基督門徒，成為祂的見証人，需要甘願冒險。

今日商業氣候中，做一個決定之前，人們習慣於先以若干方法，審慎地加以研究分析。面對耶穌的呼召，有人也試圖將祂的要求適應、吻合自己舒適的生活形態，甚至耶穌的教導都被稀釋了。事實很明了：“若有人要跟隨我，就當舍己，天天背起他的十字架，來跟隨我。”　耶穌沒有說，“你是否願意試試我的哲學系統？我的倫理法則呢？”　祂沒有像一個銷售者，也不會像一個道德家一般嘗試來說服我們，祂卻以神子的身份，面對面地與我們直接說話，全無妥協、討價還價、及談判的余地。我們跟隨的是祂的意志，不是自己的願望。耶穌明了跟隨祂的代價，這就是為什麼，祂極其鄭重地發出祂的呼召。

一個有趣的問題是，“跟隨耶穌，得益何在？”彼得曾經詢問過類似的問題（太10：27）。“我們能夠得著什麼？”答案是，永恆的生命！這是一個唯有對被選召的人才有意義的答案。在知識的層面尋覓滿意答案之前，人常試圖拖延作跟隨主的決定，為要確實地知道，跟隨耶穌究竟能得到何種回報。

請不要以商業回報的角度來決定是否跟隨耶穌。在朝聖者的旅途上，若以信心與耶穌同行，你必將覓得真正的答案。

God Listens Always

Prayer has no end, but requires an opening of the dialogue between man and God. God is delighted to hear from us. He encourages us to seek His attention, to petition Him without pause. He even appointed sentinels to remind us that He is waiting for our call always. Isaiah 62:6-7, "I have posted watchmen on your walls, O Jerusalem; they will never be silent day or night. You who call on the Lord, give yourselves no rest, and give Him no rest till He establishes Jerusalem and makes her the praise of the earth." God is saying, the work of praying is never ending on earth. He is receptive to our prayers at all times.

Luke 11:9-10, " So I say to you: Ask and it will be given to you, seek and you will find; knock and the door will be opened to you... ". We should never feel that we are asking too much of God whose storehouse of blessings is limitless. God never tires of listening to our requests. We would disappoint Him by not beseeching Him. The redemption by Christ has given us new life in love and righteousness. We are no longer the selfish creatures outside of Christ.

When we ask God, what should be our attitude? James 4:2-3, "You want something but don't get it. You kill and covet, but you cannot have what you want. You quarrel...wrong motives...". Our motives or attitudes are important when we pray.

The curse of human existence is the great deceiver who also does not rest. To help us fight against this evil, we need constant prayer as our armor. Ephesians 6:10-18, “Finally, be strong in the Lord..., Put on the full armor of God... And pray in the Spirit on all occasions with all kinds of prayers and requests..... always keep on praying for all the saints."

上帝始終垂聽

祈禱無止境，人需要開放地與神對話。

上帝喜悅垂聽人的禱告，祂鼓勵我們尋找祂的注意，無休止的向祂祈求，甚至祂委派守望者，提醒我們要不斷地向祂呼求。以賽亞書62:6-7 “耶路撒冷阿、我在你城上設立守望的．他們晝夜必不靜默。呼籲耶和華的、你們不要歇息、也不要使他歇息、直等他建立耶路撒冷、使耶路撒冷在地上成為可讚美的”。上帝說，在地上，祈禱的工作永無休止，任何時候，祂都垂聽禱告。

路加福音11:9-10 “所以，我要對你們說：你們祈求，就給你們；叩門，就給你們開門...”。不要認為自己要價太高，當知道上帝的祝福永無限量。上帝不厭其煩地聽人的祈求，不懇求的人會令上帝失望。在基督的愛和公義裡，透過救贖，祂賜下新的生命。我們不再是基督以外自私的被造者。

當我們問上帝，祈禱當持怎樣的態度？雅各書4:2-3“你們貪戀，還是得不著；你們殺害嫉妒，又鬥毆爭戰，也不能得。你們得不著，是因為你們不求。你們求也得不著，是因為你們妄求，要浪費在你們的宴樂中......”。人的祈禱，動機與態度相當重要。

人類生存最大的詛咒是那從不歇息的魔鬼。為對抗這種邪惡，我們需要不斷地披上祈禱的鎧甲。以弗所書6:10-18，“我還有末了的話：你們要靠著主，倚賴他的大能大力作剛強的人。要穿戴神所賜的全副軍裝，就能抵擋魔鬼的詭計。因我們並不是與屬血氣的爭戰（原文作摔跤；下同），乃是與那些執政的、掌權的、管轄這幽暗世界的，以及天空屬靈氣的惡魔爭戰。所以，要拿起神所賜的全副軍裝，好在磨難的日子抵擋仇敵，並且成就了一切，還能站立得住。所以要站穩了，用真理當作帶子束腰，用公義當作護心鏡遮胸，又用平安的福音當作預備走路的鞋穿在腳上。此外，又拿著信德當作籐牌，可以滅盡那惡者一切的火箭；並戴上救恩的頭盔，拿著聖靈的寶劍，就是神的道；靠著聖靈，隨時多方禱告祈求；並要在此儆醒不倦，為眾聖徒祈求”。

A Question about Salvation

There has been a long debate among Christians on the salvation of those who have not heard the gospels and therefore do not know Christ. It is a controversy which has lasted 2000 years, and is still a much debated issue. So much has been written about this subject, it would be a folly to try to present even summaries on the two sides of the argument. Arguments aside, the opposing statements are:

1. God judges righteously and justly.

2. They will go to hell.

In this article, I will briefly look into the first statement; let us call it the liberal view. We will limit our discussion to people who have not heard the gospels, not those who have heard but rejected them. We further assume that these people have accepted a God of creation who has inscribed His truth on their hearts and consciences by His revelations throughout His kingdom. So, we exclude atheists.

An obvious question to ask, before we proceed any further, is, "Why did God send His son Jesus if there are other paths for salvation?" An answer may be, Jesus is the sure way. If this is acceptable, and along with John 14:6, "I am the way, and the truth, and the life; no one comes to the Father but through Me.", we must understand Jesus' audience. He actually was referring to the people who heard him.

In support of this liberal position, many scriptural quotes have been offered to make known the merciful nature of God. Psalm 9:8 says, "And He will judge the world in righteousness; He will execute judgment for the peoples with equity." 2Peter 3:9 says,"....He is patient with you, not wanting anyone to perish, but everyone to come to repentance."... Romans 4:15 says, "For the law brings about wrath but where there is no law, neither is there violation."

It is true that no one comes to the father except through Jesus. Romans 2:14-16, ".... these, not having the law, are a law to themselves.... written in their heart, their conscience bearing witness, God will judge the secrets of men through Christ Jesus." It affirms Jesus will judge all men, those who know Him and those who don't know Him.

The conclusion of this liberal camp is this: We are judged on the basis of what we know and how we act upon it. Our conscience is ever present. For sure, we are all sinners, fallen and guilty, but Jesus will be the one and only judge who can commute our sentence. We must not presume to second-guess.

有關救恩的思考

長久以來，基督教圈子裡一個相持不下的爭論是，那些未曾聽過耶穌基督救恩的人是否能夠得救？爭論延續至今，從未中斷，很多人就此著書立論，抒發己見。此文謹將其中兩個主要觀點分析如下。

1，對未曾聽過福音的人，上帝有公平公義的判斷；

2，未曾聽過福音的人進地獄。

今天，本人願以簡潔、開明的態度，討論第一個論點。討論的對象，是那些未曾聽過福音的人，而不是那些聽過福音後拒絕相信的人。

進一步的，讓我們假設，這些人已經接受一位創造主的存在，透過救恩和啟示，神將其真理銘刻於他們的良心中。所以，此文並不牽涉無神論的討論。

其次，在未曾深入討論得救的問題之前，一個顯然的問題有待思考：如果有其他方法賜下救恩，為什麼上帝要差遣耶穌基督? 答案可以是，耶穌基督是得救恩的保証。如果此立論成立，結合約翰福音的觀點"我就是道路、真理、生命，若不藉著我，沒有人能到父那裡去"（約10：）我們當留意，耶穌說這番話的時候，他周圍站立的是一群怎樣的聽眾。

對此觀點，聖經中提供很多支持的經文，目的是解釋耶穌基督慈悲的本性--- "祂要按公義審判世界，按正直判斷萬民"(詩篇9:8)；"……不願有一人沉淪，乃願人人都悔改"(彼後3:9);"因為律法是惹動憤怒的，那裡沒有律法，那裡就沒有過犯"（羅4:15）。的確如此，離開耶穌基督，沒有人能夠到上帝那裡去。

"這是顯出律法的功用刻在他們心裡，他們是非之心同作見証，並且他們的思念互相較 量，或以為是，或以為非……"（羅2:14-16）可以肯定，耶穌將審判所有的人，包括認識祂和不認識祂的人。

此開明觀點的結語是，人受審判，是依據一個人知道甚麼，和如何反應。良心在此，人人皆有罪惡過失，但是耶穌基督是唯一一位定罪和免罪者，人不必妄自揣測。耶穌了解誰是屬他的人。對於未曾聽過福音的人，上帝自有公平公義的判斷。

Christian Motivations in Giving

Before we look into the motivations under which Christians give, we have to find out what makes people give in general. In simple terms, people try to satisfy a need, and in this case, the need to give. Why the need? The rationale is based on achieving wholeness of personality. It is for the benefit of the giver to give. At the end, the consideration may well be self-interest, even in giving. The gift is good for the community; we are a part of the community, therefore the gift is good for us. Being rewarded is a similar motivation. Some give to try to buy favor with the Almighty, and there are those who give out of a sense of guilt, the gift being a means of expiation. Returning to the need for wholeness of personality, man needs love and a sense of belonging. Giving is a means of expressing affection as well as securing it. Let us not be cynical, genuine affection must find tangible means of expressing itself, and this frequently takes the form of gift. We are transitioning from the self to altruism.

Christian giving is not mutually exclusive to the sociological or psychological motivations mentioned above.

The Old Testament suggests that gifts to God as sacrifice are a reminder that everything belongs to the Lord. Sacrifice expressed gratitude, repentance, and sharing a relationship with God. This began to move away from the idea that man is utterly a selfish creature. Jesus did not define giving in terms of response of our love towards His love. He was very down to earth:

"Give to the poor, and you will have treasure in heaven." (Mark 10:21)

"For the measure you give will be the measure you get back." (Luke 6:38)

He accepted the idea of reward, but elevated it to a higher plane. He made the intimate connection between love and giving when He asked Peter, "Do you love me?", "Feed my sheep." (John 2:15-17). Giving must be a genuine expression of love. Paul insisted that love expresses itself in giving (2Cor 8:8-9). He did not apologize for the expectation of rewards in giving (2Cor 9:6).

Let us examine some of the specific motivations in Christian giving.

Gratitude is the awareness of God's mercy. We do not thank God for a list of gifts. It is a relationship with the Giver, so that even if the gifts were to disappear, our relation with God is intact. We are members of God's family. Our service to our brethren is the expression of our gratitude to God. Love from God in creation and redemption calls forth love. Stewardship of giving responds to God's love. In the relationship of love, giving is a major component. Christian giving is the response of love to love. Obedience is a pious action not stipulated by law. it is doing what is consistent with God's spirit and purpose. The Christian wants to do His will. It is a voluntary obedience. God's purpose in caring for His creation and therefore His people, is strong motivation for us to share in this care by giving to others. In many places of the NT, the idea of reward was plainly expressed. There needs to be no shame in looking forward to rewards as completion of salvation. The reward of love may well be a greater capacity to love.

Paul Tillich wrote, " Religion is, first, an open hand to receive a gift and second, an acting hand to distribute gifts." 2 Corinthians 10:7-8 tells us:

"Each man should give what he has decided in his heart to give, not reluctantly or under compulsion, for God loves a cheerful giver. And God is able to make all grace abound to you so that in all things at all times, having all that you need, you will abound in every good work."

基督徒奉獻的動機

在討論基督徒奉獻的動機之前，我們需要了解一個人願意施予的原因。

簡單來說，當人們希望滿足一個需要，他們會為這個需要而獻上。施予的原理和動機基於自我人格的整全，　著眼於施予者本人的好處，如此的施予，徹頭徹尾的是基於個人的興趣。

作為群體的一員，能夠為群體獻上固然使人得益，但獻上的同時，我們自己同樣得益。為人格的整全而施與，同樣也是因為愛和相屬感，施予表達的是情感和信心。

不必玩世不恭，情感的表達，未必有可見的途徑。但是至少，施予，將人由自我為中心中抽離，轉向為他人的好處設想。

有些人施予是為自己的負疚感向全能者買單，將所獻上的當做補償。

另外一些人施予的動機，是基於有所回報。

基督徒的給予並不排除上述社會和心理的動因。

舊約獻祭物給神，目的是提醒人凡物神屬：一切皆出於神、最終要歸於神。獻上祭物所要表達的是感恩，悔改，和分享神人關系。透過所奉獻祭物，人知道，自己不再是自私的被造物。

新約中，耶穌沒有為所獻上的做界定，而施予的原則卻是：借給窮人的，是借給造他的主，是積攢財寶在天上（可10:21）。耶穌說，“你們用甚麼量器量給人，也必用甚麼量器量給你們”（路6:38）。耶穌沒有否定回報的說法，但耶穌將之昇華。當祂詢問彼得的時候，他問：“你愛我嗎？-----你牧養我的羊”（約2:15-17）。愛和施予被昇華到一種和神更為緊密的關系裡面。

施予是愛最真誠的表達，使徒保羅有同樣的洞見(林後8:8-9),在施予的理論中，他所強調的其中一個重點就是施比受更為有福。(林後9:6)

在基督徒的奉獻方面，我們可以由如下幾方面來檢測自己的動機----

是否出於感恩？我們感恩不僅是因為所得到的，更是與賜予者的關系，感恩是基於對神憐憫的醒悟。可見的物質可以消失，但和造物主的關係毫發無損。我們是神家裡的成員，透過服侍手足表達對父神的感恩。

是否基於愛？神創造和救贖的大愛催促我們去愛，而愛最直接的表達是奉獻。順服不是因為律法的要求，乃是因愛神而產生的、與神的心意、目的相協調的內在的願望，爲愛神、行神的旨意而引發的內心的順服。神對我們的心意，是照料祂手所造的，顧念屬祂的子民,而與眾分享恰恰反應了我們願意順服的心意。

賞賜在哪裡？新約很多有關賞賜的記錄，在永世當中，救恩成就的日子，神必有賞賜，那是因愛而來的賞賜！神學家保羅田立克說，“宗教，就是一方面伸手接受，另一方面揮手施與。”

“各人要隨本心所籌定的，不要作難、不要勉強。因為捐得樂意的人，是神所喜愛的。神能將各樣的恩惠多多的加給你們，使你們凡事常常充足，能多行各樣善事。”---林後10:7-8。

Church Order and Church Spirit

Much scholarly writing has been devoted to the conformation or the shape of the church in the world. This concept means more than church organization or government. It has to do with the will of Christ who is its head. Christian believers gather together into church order to affect a behavior in the spirit of Christ to all men, as members of the family of God. They have the responsibility for ensuring that the life and work of His people are carried forward in the world. Preaching the WORD and administration of the sacraments by qualified ministers are givens. The church must engage in evangelism, mutual care, and compassionate outreach. Proper expression and functioning in these responsibilities require church order and church spirit.

History shows the necessity of some church order, but it is important that it should not be too rigid. Form must not submerge substance. Christ's work should not be bound tightly to such a form. Some churches have been accused of subordinating Christ to the church, in which the forms have overtaken Christ's claim to be master of His own house.

The church must embody the services of the Body of Christ among men, reflecting the life and passion of Jesus. The church is a servant of the divine initiative. Many churches lack visible church order. Yet, as long as Christ finds room in such churches, we cannot deny their Christian pedigree.

Perhaps a good analogy for the living church order can be found in the metaphor of an army on the march. The purpose of the church order is to ensure the people of God are moving towards their true destination, the reconciliation crafted by Christ. Our purpose is not perfecting the organization which is temporary. The church order is not a monument which keeps the spirit confined within man-made bounds. We should not settle into a rigid muscle-bound order. We must pay attention to the spirit of the eternal home and not the secular roots.

Church order has been known to be used as tools of personal ambition leading to pettiness worse than those of the world about the churches. This has led some people to repudiate the church even when they acknowledge some validity in the teaching of Christ. They speak of the betrayal of Christ by the churches. Let us pray that the Spirit will always lead us.

教會規例與精神

很多討論有關教會當以何種形態處世的學術作品，其觀念不僅指教會的結構和管理，更關係到教會之首耶穌基督對教會的心意。基督徒來到教會，當體現基督精神，並使之成為上帝的家。

信徒的責任是要將耶穌的生活和工作向前推廣；而聖職人員則忠心傳揚真理，實施聖禮；教會當委身傳福音，彼此相愛，發揮外展的熱忱。切實表達教會功能，不但需要生活和工作的規章，還需要教會精神的配合。

歷史証實了這一點，教會需要規章,其關鍵當避免過度刻板。教會事工不當受形式枷鎖的束縛，其內在的真實不能被外在的形式所代替，重規章甚於耶穌的精神。

教會，乃耶穌基督在人群中的具體表現，反映著耶穌的生命和熱忱，是上帝的居所。很多教會雖然沒有明顯的規章，但若耶穌在當中居住，就不能夠否認這不是基督的教會。

教會規例和精神可作如下比較：一個滿有活力的教會，如同正在行進中的軍隊。其規章的目的，是保証上帝子民以合一的姿態，向正確的目標行進。教會規例是暫時的，不是一個人為的紀念碑，結構是否十全十美不是最重要的。教會的組織和結構不當受世俗規例的轄制，使之遮蔽其內在的精神。教會精神讓人留意的，當是永恆的家園。

教會規例有時被人利用為私人的工具來達致一己野心，較外面的世界更甚、更令人反感。雖然信仰的美善得到承認，但如斯光景，必成為人們攻擊教會的口實，指責教會利用規例、出賣上帝的家。惟願聖靈幫助並帶領我們免此錯誤。

Discipleship: Our Retreat

We took a leap of faith when we asked to be baptized. We made a decision. Perhaps we did not fully understand that it was only the first step in a progression of unending steps towards Jesus, to become more like Him. It is one thing to learn about Christ, quite another to act with Him in you, to walk in His way. It is not just the intellect, it demands heart. This is the reason for retreats. They are our pit-stops for spiritual refueling. It is a time to rediscover the excitement and the zeal that invited you to meet Jesus in the first place. The theme of our retreat is:

Discipleship, Rise and Let Your Light Shine.

Let us look into what these key words means.

Discipleship means to do as Christ taught, summed up by "if anyone would come after me, he must deny himself and take up his cross and follow me". We are asked to be proactive followers, not just admiring spectators.

Rise means to stand up for Christ, to be unashamed as a follower. Paul said: "For I am not ashamed of the gospel, it is the power of God for salvation to everyone who has faith" (Romans 1:16). Will you stand up for the Lord when all about you are chiding you? Will you still claim the Lord when the world taunts His words? Will you give an answer to everyone who asks you to give the reason for the hope that you have? (1Peter3:5). Rise and walk in faith, keeping a clear conscience so that those who speak maliciously against your good behavior in Christ may be ashamed of their slander.

Light Shine means to love one another as Jesus has loved you (John13:34) and to make disciples of all nations (Matt 28:19). Love your fellowmen and share the light of Jesus with them. You are the light of the world. (Matt5:14) Let your light shine before men. (Matt5:16)

Let us join hands this time of the year, to celebrate Discipleship in our retreat in the peacefulness of natural surroundings. Come and share a spiritual expedition.

興起！發光！作門徒！
教會退修會

最初決定洗禮歸主的時候，我們已經跨出信心旅程的第一步，或者當時未必意識到這僅僅是第一步。我們仍需要走近基督，並且越來越像祂。知道耶穌，僅屬於認知的層面，我們還需要有因基督的內在而發自內心的行動，這就是教會組織退修會的目的。退修會是我們靈性進步的加油站，再次發掘我們的熱心和奮興，再次重溫與主首次相遇的美好經歷。

教會今年退修會的主題是：興起，發光！作門徒！意義何在？

“做門徒”，即是實踐耶穌的教導，越來越像祂。綜歸就是耶穌所說的：“若有人要跟隨我，就當舍己，背起他的十字架來跟隨我。”主要求我們做跟隨者，而非旁觀者。

“興起”，為耶穌挺身而出，不以福音為恥。

保羅說:“我不以福音為恥，這福音本是神的大能，要救一切相信的”(羅1:16)。你是否願意為主挺身而出？當身邊的人恥笑你，你是否還承認你的主？當有人問如何得著盼望，你將如何作答？興起為耶穌！持守清潔的良心，敵對者將頓感羞愧。

“發光”，要愛人如同主愛你（約13:34），要使萬人作門徒，與人分享基督的真光。我們是世上的光，我們的光當照在人前。

讓我們手牽手，與弟兄姐妹一同到一個寧靜天然的退修營地，去進行一次靈性的探險！

Earning the Right

Back in September of 2005, on the first day of school, Martha Cothren, a social studies school teacher at Robinson High School in Little Rock , did something not to be forgotten. On the first day of school, with the permission of the school superintendent, the principal and the building supervisor, she removed all of the desks out of her classroom. When the first period kids entered the room they discovered that there were no desks.

"Ms. Cothren, where are our desks?"

She replied, "You can't have a desk until you tell me how you earn the right to sit at a desk."

They thought, "Well, maybe it's our grades."

"No," she said.

"Maybe it's our behavior."

She told them, "No, it's not even your behavior."

And so, they came and went, the first period, second period, third period. Still no desks in the classroom. By early afternoon television news crews had started gathering in Ms. Cothren's classroom to report about this crazy teacher who had taken all the desks out of her room. The final period of the day came and as the puzzled students found seats on the floor of the deskless classroom, Martha Cothren said, "Throughout the day no one has been able to tell me just what he or she has done to earn the right to sit at the desks that are ordinarily found in this classroom. Now I am going to tell you."

At this point, Martha Cothren went over to the door of her classroom and opened it.

Twenty-seven (27) U.S. Veterans, all in uniforms, walked into that classroom, each one carrying a school desk. The Vets began placing the school desks in rows, and then they would walk over and stand alongside the wall. By the time the last soldier had set the final desk in place those kids started to understand, perhaps for the first time in their lives, just how the right to sit at those desks had been earned.

Martha said, "You didn't earn the right to sit at these desks. These heroes did it for you. They placed the desks here for you. Now, it's up to you to sit in them. It is your responsibility to learn, to be good students, to be good citizens. They paid the price so that you could have the freedom to get an education. Don't ever forget it. "

By the way, this is a true story. And this teacher was awarded Teacher of the Year for the state of Arkansas in 2006.

Can we relate this story to our right to be God's children? Who earned this right for us?

如何贏得權利？

瑪莎卡倫，一個在羅賓遜高中學校作社會研究的老師， 於2005年9月開學的第一天，經校監、校長和主管的許可，做了一件令人難以忘懷的事。當學生進來上課的時候，他們發現教室裡面沒有書桌。瑪莎卡倫將所有的課桌都搬了出去。

“卡倫女士，我們的課桌在哪裡呢？”

卡倫回答說，“除非你能告訴我，你如何得著能夠坐在一張書桌前的權利，否則，你不能有一張書桌。”

“嗯……或許是因為我們的年級。”

“不，”她說。

“又或許是因為我們的行為。”

“不，它根本不關行為的事。”

於是，學生來了又走了，第一班、第二班、第三班……教室裏依然沒有課桌。

下午，教室裏聚集著電視新聞工作人員，報告這位將課桌搬出教室、不可理喻的卡倫女士。

這一天，當最後一班迷糊不解的學生，進到這個無課桌、需要坐在地板上的課室的時候，瑪莎卡倫女士開腔了：“整整一天，都沒有人能夠告訴我，他/她究竟如何獲得坐在這間教室課桌旁的權利。現在就讓我來告訴你。”在這當兒，瑪莎卡倫走過去，打開了教室的大門。

赫然看見24位美國退伍軍人，每人攜帶著一個課桌，著裝整齊地走了進來。將課桌一行行的排好之後，他們就走去站在牆邊。當最後一位士兵，將最後一張課桌放好的時候，學生們開始明白，生命中第一次知道，他們坐在課桌旁的權利是如何賺來的……

瑪莎卡倫說，“若沒有這些英雄，你們就沒有坐在課桌旁的權利。現在，你們可以坐在這裡，得著受教育的自由，但你們有責任努力向學，成為好學生、好公民，因為這些英雄曾經為之付上代價。請你們謹記。”

在這個真實故事的尾聲，這位老師被授予2006年阿肯色州年度教師獎。

透過這個故事，我們當反省，又是誰，為我們贏得作上帝兒女的權利呢？

The Better Followers of Jesus

Blaise Pascal: Knowledge and Faith

Most of us do not know much about Blaise Pascal of the 17th century. He was a brilliant scientist and philosopher, a critic of Descartes. A good introduction to Pascal may be what the twelfth century theologian, St. Anselm, said : "I believe that I may understand; I do not understand that I may believe."

This quotation reminds us that human intellect in limited. That reason alone can reveal all is suspect. Has reason explained the existence of matter? Reason, analysis, and science are wonderful gifts of God to understand the natural laws governing His creation. I am no philosopher and cannot even claim to be a student. I happen to come across some thoughts of Blaise Pascal, who was known to me only as a scientist and a mathematician. He is celebrated by the use of his name in scientific pressure units, the Pascal. In fact, to my ignorance, he was a child prodigy of the 17th century and was a noted philosopher. He proposed a famous wager, the Pascal Wager, using mathematical reasoning to try to persuade the agnostic with the conclusion:

"Belief (in God) is a wise wager. Granted that faith cannot be proved, what harm will come to you if you gamble on its truth and it proves false? If you gain, you gain all; if you lose, you lose nothing. Wager, then, without hesitation, that He (God) exists."

His analysis gave rise to decision theory and added much to the field of probability. He saw the limitation of man in the scheme of the infinite: For after all what is man in nature? A nothing in relation to infinity, all in relation to nothing, a central point between nothing and all and infinity, far from understanding either. The ends of things and their beginnings are impregnably concealed from him in an impenetrable secret. He is equally incapable of seeing the nothingness out of which he was drawn and the infinite in which he is engulfed.

He did not disparage reason but he was wise enough to include the heart:

"We know the truth not only through our reason but also through our heart.....For knowledge, of first principles, like space, time, motion, numbers, is as solid as any derived through reason, and it is on such knowledge, coming from the heart and instinct, that reason has to depend and base all its arguments."

" That is why those to whom God has given religious faith by moving their hearts are very fortunate....but to those who do not have it we can only give such faith through reasoning, until God gives it by moving their heart, without which faith is only human and useless for salvation."

Pascal's notion that knowledge does not come from reason alone, but also from the heart, stands us in good stead with God.

The Better Followers of Jesus

畢雷斯帕司考----知識和信心

畢雷斯帕司考或者鮮為人知。他是17世紀著名的科學家和哲學家，曾經批判過大名鼎鼎的笛卡爾。若要恰當地介紹此人，可借用12世紀神學家聖安瑟倫的話："信而知，非知而信。"

聖安瑟倫的話提醒人類，智商是有限制的，僅憑理智與邏輯解釋事物是當受質疑的，理智不能解釋物質的存在。理智、分析、與科學乃是上帝所賜的禮物，為向人闡述大自然的規律，如何善用與管理。

本人並非哲學家，接觸帕司考的思想實屬巧合。原以為他是一位科學家和數學家，因為"帕司考"（Pascal）其名原為科學上一個壓力的單位，後來才知此人乃17世紀的天才少年及科學家，不禁為一己無知而汗顏。

為了令未曾聽過福音的人相信上帝，帕司考嘗試以數學分析的方式來令人歸主。他承認，科學不能証實信心。但是，選擇是否相信上帝，恰如一個聰明的賭博。如果上帝不存在，賭博輸了，又有何妨？人沒有任何損失；但是若果上帝存在，人會贏得盤滿缽滿！一賭又何妨！

帕司考的理論最終令【判斷的理論】問世，對之有興趣的科學家趨之若鶩，後來更在其發明的"可能"的領域裡，注入了更豐富的內涵與知識。

相對廣大和無限，帕司考洞悉人的有限。他認為，"在大自然的無限裡，人祇是無有；然而在無有裡，人是所有。"人祇是佇立於無限和無有當中的一個"點"，但是人既不了解無限，也不明白無有；人不能洞悉初始，也不能解釋終結，這些領域都是人不能進入的奧秘。人來自無有，故人不能了解無有；人置於無限當中，故人也看不見無限。

帕司考並不輕視理智， 但他將心智融入理智。他認為，對真理的了解，不僅僅因為理智，也因為一顆心。理智和心所知道的，諸如空間、時間、數字……仿佛理智一般，既實在、又有價值。單憑理智是不夠的，理智原由知識和心而出。這就是為什麼上帝將福音賜予有信心之人。祇有理智和理由，卻缺乏知識和心性，與救恩無補。

帕司考相信，知識並非僅僅出自理智，還需要心的配合，如此，才能進入上帝裡面。

The Better Followers of Jesus

Just a Good Man?

Many good men, great men, irresistible teachers have impressed us in history. Was Jesus one of them such that he should command our admiration and perhaps our allegiance? Was there something unique about him that set him apart from "good men"? It has been documented that his character, his teaching, his behavior, his abilities, his fulfillment of prophecy, and his claims all add up to more than a good man. His contemporaries believed he was one with God. Let us look at just one area of his difference----his claims.

The gospels record him as a very humble person teaching the people, befriending the outcasts, healing the sick, and mixing with sinners. He was a low-keyed carpenter with earthy wisdom. Yet, he made the most fantastic claims. He would use names for himself which the Jews had always reserved for deity: "I am", Son of Man, the good shepherd.

Jesus offered no apology that he was entitled to man's worship, that due to God (Luke 5:8). Peter cried out to him, "Depart from me, for I am a sinful man, Master." Jesus took it in stride (John 20:28). Thomas burst out, after the resurrection, "my Lord, and my God." Jesus was not fazed. Would any good man conduct himself in that manner? Good men like Peter and Paul remonstrated when some people tried to worship them. Jesus said, "Your sins are forgiven you," to a woman caught in adultery. The learned Pharisees knew exactly what it meant. Who is this that forgives sins?

I paraphrase C. S. Lewis: In the light of His life and His fantastic claims, what can we say? If you are stuck for words, then maybe the way He died and the way He rose from the dead would convince you of Paul's conclusion, "He was declared to be Son of God."

純粹好人？

歷史上無數的好人、偉人、及無可抗拒的教師留給我們無比深刻的印象。耶穌是否其中的一員，值得我們景仰跟隨呢？相對其他“好人”,祂有何獨特之處？縱觀耶穌的性格、教訓、行為、能力、其預言的應驗、及其宣稱的記錄，可以知道，祂絕非僅僅是個好人。與祂同代的人相信祂與上帝合一，祂就是上帝。祂的宣稱，展示着祂與眾不同的一面。

福音書記錄的耶穌是個十分謙卑的人。祂教導人，醫治人，與被棄的人作朋友，甚至與罪人在一起。祂是個低調的木匠，有平易近人的智慧。祂以猶太人用來稱呼神的的方法，發出許多了不起的宣稱---“我是”，“神子”，“好牧人”。

祂從不為自己被冠以神之名、受人敬拜而道歉（路5:8)。彼得呼喊說：“主啊，離開我吧，我是個罪人!”耶穌對此受之無愧（約20:28)；復活後，多馬說“我的主、我的神”，耶穌認為此乃理所當然之稱謂，而普通人是不會輕易接受如此稱呼的。比如，當有人欲崇拜彼得和保羅的時候，他們曾極力抗拒。後來，耶穌對一個通奸被捉的婦人說：“你的罪赦了”的時候，博學的法力賽人深諳耶穌的用意,禁不住自忖，這個人是誰？竟赦免人的罪？

C.S.Lewis說，在基督生命的光中，在其偉大的宣稱裡，人無話可說，無言以對。祂的死、祂的復活，論証了保羅的話，说：“祂被稱為上帝的兒子”。

Stewardship and Church Business I

Business is about having a good product or service that people will buy. From this kernel, the whole theater of microeconomics and business school concepts has flowered. Are there any parallel or anti-parallels between economic business and the spiritual business of our church?

What is our product or service? Our tangible product is the Gospel of Jesus Christ. Our service is to explain Jesus' message to those near and far. We are not the owners of our business, but are the managers or stewards who have been entrusted to bring fruit by working with the assets, protecting them and expanding them while generating a spiritual return. A visible distinguishing mark is that we are simultaneously the management and the customers.

We have been charged with an investment dating back 2000 years. Ordinary business might call it an intangible asset or goodwill because it is today not a physical or material asset. To us, however, it is true and tangible history. Here is a catch.

Practically all business goodwill is written off with time, i.e., amortized to zero as time passes. Quite the contrary, our goodwill from Jesus Christ has grown with time. We have an asset that does not die. Its value cannot be measured in dollars. It is infinite. This fact makes any discussion of return on investment meaningless.

Like other businesses, we are concerned with income and expense. While the expense side can be fairly objectively addressed, given the decisions of church leaders to apply our resources to a prayerfully prioritized list of activities, we are left with finding the resources to support our chosen ministries. There is a Chinese saying, "eat a quantity of rice to match the dishes on the table." Sadly this ancient wisdom cannot be simply adopted in our church work.

God has mandated our work. We cannot quit God's work if we are true followers of Christ. A famous song offers this lyrical line in our context: try when your arms are too weary. We must try. We came into this world with nothing except the gift of life. We shall leave with nothing except the grace of God. All the material riches are but temporary free credit from God.

Other than for our worldly obligations, we must return our possessions to the name of the Creditor, in His service. Our possessions include our time and talents. While we try to walk in Jesus' footsteps, we open our hearts and material bounty to serve and glorify God. We seek no returns for ourselves. Our stewardship reflects our joy not our burden. It is both a practical and a symbolic act to help lighten the cross. Remember the poor widow at the synagogue? Let us pray that all of us give in sincerity. Know that our wealth can heal or hurt.

Mathew 6:24 says "No one can serve two masters. Either he will hate the one and love the other, or he will be devoted to the one and despise the other. You cannot serve both God and money".

Every one of us is a steward in the house of the Lord.

管家與教會經營

商業貿易所論及的是如何令顧客樂意光顧良好的產品和優質的服務。由此核心出發，微型經濟學和商業學校對於經營管理的概念就被發揮的更顯絢麗。問題在於，商業經營和教會靈性的經營是否有異曲同工之處呢？長老會的資產和服務又是什麼呢？

我們最寶貴的資產就是耶穌基督的福音，教會的服務就是將福音的好處傳給近處和遠處的人。我們不是這盤生意的主人，乃是受托的管家，透過經營、保護和拓展這寶貴的資產，獲得屬靈的回報。作為基督徒，顯而易見，我們兼任着兩個角色--既是管理者，又是顧客。

兩千年至今，基督徒都被賦予投資的責任。一般商家認為投資不僅僅指有形的物質，也包含了無形的資產及商譽價值。對基督徒來說，屬靈的投資是透過時間及可見的歷史，這就是其中的蹊蹺。實際上，所有的商業信譽都會逐漸降低，甚至隨時間流逝而注銷報廢。唯有教會的信譽卻因耶穌基督的福音與日俱增，其價值無遠弗屆，遠非金錢所能衡量，福音的資產永不消亡，讓世上所謂的投資回報率變得黯然失色。

與所有經營一樣，教會也會考慮收入和支出。支出部分一目了然，提醒教會當根據本身的現狀，透過禱告來部署各種活動的優先次序。但是，我們需要進一步發掘賴以支持教會事工的屬靈資源。中國古代的智慧說"睇餸食飯"，是不适合被教會採纳的。上帝賦予我們管家的權力，請不要放棄這個權力。

有首充滿激情的詩歌說 "繼續嘗試！即使你的雙臂感到倦怠"，我們必須去嘗試。除了上帝所賜予的生命，我們沒有帶什麼到世上來；除了將上帝的恩典留下，我們也不會從世上帶走任何的東西。所有的好處和豐富都是上帝免費的借貸，有朝一日我們需要向貸方交賬。

上帝賜予我們的包括了時間和才干，當我們立志跟隨耶穌基督的腳蹤，必會樂意將身心獻上、將所擁有的獻上，去回報和榮耀上帝。不要單為自己尋求回報，管家的職分帶給我們的是喜樂，而不是重軛；透過實在的奉獻和具體的行動來舒緩神家財政的負擔。讓我們祈願每個人都能夠誠心的施予，不要忘記，財能載舟，也能覆舟。

馬太福音6；24耶穌對我們的提醒是這樣的"一個人不能事奉兩個主，不是惡這個，愛那個，就是重這個輕那個。你們不能又事奉神，又事奉瑪門（財利）。"

請不要忘記，你是神的管家！

The Better Followers of Jesus

Stewardship and Church Business II

Christians are not bound by the Jewish tithing laws but early Christians were generous in helping each other. The apostle Paul spoke out clearly on the subject.

"The disciples, each according to his ability, decided to provide help...." ; ".....were pleased to make a contribution for the poor among the saints in Jerusalem. They were pleased to do it,...." ; "....On the first day of every week, each one of you should set aside a sum of money in keeping with his income, saving it up....". (Acts 11:29-30, Rom 15:26-28, 1 Cor. 16:1).

He gave no fixed rule about percentages but told each person to give what he could afford. The call is for generosity in giving.

We are stewards in God's house. We are charged with maintaining and growing the church. As a voluntary organization, our church obviously needs contributions from its members to carry on its ministries. An often quoted passage comes from Malachi 3:8-10, "....because you are robbing me. Bring the whole tithe into the storehouse, that there may be food in my house....".

Our church asks members to pledge their annual estimated donation for good planning. The response has not been encouraging. Our church finances have suffered losses for a number of years. Regular contribution simply have not covered normal expenses.

Please remember that every one of us is a steward.

再論管家

基督徒的奉獻不是因為舊約律法的約束,乃是始於上帝的恩典和初代基督徒真誠的互助。

使徒保羅說:"門徒定意照各人的力量捐錢,去供給住在猶太的弟兄"(徒11:29-30); "我往耶路撒冷去供給聖徒,因為馬其頓和亞該亞人樂意湊出捐項給耶路撒冷聖徒中的窮人"(羅15:26-28);

"每逢七日的第一日各人要照自己的進項抽出來留著,免得我來的時候現湊"(林前16:12)。

在他的書信中，保羅沒未規定基督徒奉獻的比例是多少，但他鼓勵人當慷慨地向神獻上。

瑪拉基書3章8-10說:"人豈可奪取神之物呢?以色列人竟在當納的十分之一和當獻的供物上,奪取神的供物。"

我們是神的管家，　負責教會的維繫和增長。作為一個志願的團體,教會很需要會友在財政方面支持神的事工。教會希望每個會友都能夠交上個人奉獻的預算，為的是幫助教會安排來年的聖工,我們有待大家的響應，因為過去多年，教會飽受財政拘拮據之苦，很多時候甚至入不敷出。

財政問題不是今天才發生的，會友流失，多年的經濟不景氣和利息減低一直影響著過去幾年教會的收入。　我盼望每個人都成為神殿中慷慨的管家。

The Subtle Sin

Most of us do not recognize a serious vice which infects just about everyone. Yet, everyone is revolted when they see it in someone else. Exhibition of this vice creates ill will among men. It is a social sin as well as an affront to God. We are most of the time unconscious of it in ourselves, but the more we have it ourselves, the more we dislike it in others. The sin is pride, the antithesis of Christian humility. C.S. Lewis calls it the complete anti-God state of mind.

It is a fact that the more pride one has, the more one dislikes pride in others. Ask yourself, how much do I hate it when other people do not take notice of me? Pride competes and adds jealousy to the mix. Pride gets no pleasure from possessing something, but only out of having more of it than others. Comparison feeds your pride, the pleasure of being above the rest, the inner desire to show superiority. The proud man may have more than what he can use, but he wants more just to assert his power. This applies not only to material things but in the intellectual and spiritual realms.

Pride has been the chief cause of misery since the world began. It always produces enmity, not only among men but enmity to God. Your pride stops you from knowing God. Even in churches, those infected with pride can appear to be very religious. They imagine God approves and agrees that they are better than others.

Pride is to be distinguished from the pleasure one gets when others praise you for a job well done. The pleasure comes from your having pleased others. The trouble begins when you pass from thinking, "I have done well for my fellowmen," to" what a fine person I must be."

On another plane, pride gives yourself the credit for something that God has accomplished. The credit and glory belong to God. The proud are so consumed with themselves that their thoughts are far from God. Pride is self-worshipping. Satan was cast out of heaven because of pride.

Let us not seek glory for ourselves when we serve God's church.

微妙的罪

有一種幾乎影響所有人，但又被很多人忽略，唯當在別人身上看見它的時候，我們才會嗤之以鼻的惡習。這種惡習的影響盡人皆知，既是一種社會的敗壞，也是對上帝的不恭。很多時候我們或者渾然不知，但透過他人，我們看見它的存在。這，就是驕傲---基督徒謙卑的對立面。C.S Lewis（魯益師）稱之為,"全然抵擋神的精神狀態。"

事實是，一個人越是驕傲，就越反感他人的驕傲。試問，當一個人被忽視的時候，對他人驕傲反感的程度將會如何？驕傲實在是競爭與嫉妒的組合。擁有多，並不構成驕傲；祇有自以為比他人更多，才會產生驕傲。攀比助長驕傲，高人一等、趾高氣揚令驕傲變本加厲。驕傲之人，擁有的比實際需要的更多，為的是要確定個人的權力。驕傲不僅適用於物質方面，智力和精神層面的驕傲亦俯首皆是。

由世界的初始，驕傲就是引致苦難的罪魁禍首。驕傲令人樹敵無數，不僅在人與人之間制造麻煩，也令神人疏離，徒添敵意。驕傲阻擋了人對上帝的認識。即使在教會裡，驕傲也可以身披虔誠現於人前；他們臆測，上帝對其優越感是認可的。

驕傲與因工作出色，得到他人讚美時時內心所產生的歡愉之情截然不同。因為這種欣喜是基於他人接納而產生的歡樂情感。驕傲則始於沾沾自喜與自我陶醉，過度自詡："我實在是眾人的福星"，或者"我是無懈可擊的"。

另一方面，驕傲，令我們搶奪當歸給上帝的稱讚和榮耀，令我們遠離上帝，自我中心，自我崇拜。撒旦正是因著驕傲被神趕出天庭的啊！

我們切不可祇尋求一己的榮耀，當謙卑的服務上帝和祂的教會。

Gambling Is Allowed?

It is widely accepted that gambling carried to extremes or addiction poses a serious sociological problem. This is why laws exist to contain this activity. We hear warning in the media to remind us about the dangers of gambling. From the perspective of Christianity, we address a quite different issue in fundamental terms. Is gambling prohibited by Christian doctrine? What is the moral dimension?

We must first define gambling. Gambling means games of chance in which the primary objective in for winners to profit from losers. Betting stakes are involved. So, the same games when played with no money are not gambling. Gambling can also be viewed as experiments in the respected intellectual field of probability.

The bible actually says very little about gambling. Often, the story of the Roman soldiers casting lots to see who would get Christ's robe is cited for the condemnation of gambling. That actually was not gambling according to our definition.

Christians believe that one should not try to gain at the expense of one's neighbors. Therefore, gambling with a view to gain from neighbors is unchristian. This leads us to the question of motivation or attitude. Think about a game of golf or bowling among friends for money. It certainly intensifies the excitement or fun. Here, skill is involved, not just chance. If we look at it this way, the primary objective is fun and fellowship, while the money is just an aid. So, having a stake or bet is not necessarily bad.

Let us move onto a more familiar pastime, mah-jong, played by many Chinese. When played as a social activity among friends, the objective is again fellowship and fun. In a way, we can equate it to golf or bowling where skill plays a part. The ups and downs do not break anyone in such friendly games and fellowship is enjoyed all around. There is a saying among such players, "the stake money rotates among the pockets of the players in the long term." So, there is little profiteering at the expense of one's neighbors. Viewed this way, the game is not unchristian.

When any game acquires as its primary motivation, the injury of one's neighbors for one's own gain, we have an entirely different picture. There is no positivity to it. The attitude is unchristian. For Christians, the attempt to get something for nothing at the expense of others is wrong. It is a wish for undeserved gain while others lose. This principle might be applied to church bingo or lottery. However, people forget that in playing these games, as long as winning is an element of fun while the stakes are considered donations, we are not guilty of profiting from our neighbors' expense. Again, it boils down to attitude.

We can see that there is no unambiguous line of moral determination. We have to consider motivation, attitude, skill, and consequences. The best guide is the bible's view of money, greed, and love of neighbors. It is not a case of codified law, set in stone.

The Better Followers of Jesus

賭博被許可嗎？

極端或成癮的賭博， 被廣泛認為是一個嚴重的社會問題。這就是為什麼此項活動不僅受法律管制，媒體也一再警告提醒人賭博的危害。由基督教的角度出發，其教義是否禁止賭博？道德的層面又如何？

首先，何謂賭博？賭博是指基於機會的遊戲，為贏或輸作投注，贏者從輸者身上獲利。沒有錢的投注不是賭博，乃瞭無殺傷力的遊戲。賭博也可以被視為智商領域中可能性的研究。

事實上，聖經甚少論及賭博。有關譴責賭博的記錄，是羅馬士兵如何抽籤，得到基督長袍的故事。事實上，這並不是今天所定義的賭博。

基督徒認為，人們不當試圖以犧牲他人來獲利。因此，由他人身上得利的賭博並非基督徒的作為，關乎動機或態度的問題。試想若干朋友參加高爾夫球或保齡球的比賽，賭錢，無疑增添了樂趣。但是當中技能的樂趣，遠非所賭之錢能够代替，如此賭博並非僅僅是偶然的輸贏，主要目標是樂趣和團契，金錢衹是一種添加劑。金錢牽涉其中的游戲, 並非全然丑恶。

再看一個更熟悉的消遣：許多中國人玩的麻將。麻將作為朋友間的社交活動，目的是團契與樂趣，與高爾夫球或保齡球等同，皆是技能發揮的游戲。輸贏並不破壞彼此間的情誼。球員間曾有一種說法，“賭注的錢，拿出來後衹能輪流裝入各人口袋中。”所以，甚少在鄰居身上獲得暴利。由此角度來看，麻將並不僅是非基督徒的游戲。

當一種游戲以損人利己為目的時候，情況就截然相反了，不俱任何的正面性。對於基督徒，犧牲他人，謀求獲利純屬不勞而獲，損人利己。教堂裏的數字抽獎遊戲，贏者得著樂趣，輸者不是損失，乃是捐贈，並非由他人的口袋中獲利，此乃態度的表達。

由此，我們看到，賭博並沒有一條明確的道德界線，主要在乎動機、態度、技能與後果。沒有甚麼篆刻下來的明文規定，最好的指南當屬【聖經】有關金錢、貪婪、與愛鄰居的原則。

From the Diary of a Centurion

I recently came across a small book, which is a dramatization, of the eye-witnessing by a centurion in command at Christ's crucifixion. What he saw and heard sums up the essential Christ. I would like to share the legend of Longinus' intimate experience with Jesus, here with you.

Being the centurion on that First Good Friday, Longinus heard these "Seven Words":

1. Father, forgive them for they know not what they do.
2. Verily I say unto thee, today shall thou be with me in paradise.
3. Woman, behold thy son…behold thy mother!
4. My God, My God, why hast thou forsaken me?
5. I thirst.
6. It is finished.
7. Father, into thy hands, I commend my spirit.

While each utterance deserves a thorough theological discussion, here we will simply describe how some of these words changed Longinus' life.

He thought he had seen all manners of prisoners condemned to be crucified: the whiners, the cursers, the criers for mercy, and the blasphemers, but he never saw one like the Nazarene who said gently, "Father, forgive them, for they know not what they do." Unbelievable! Jesus was more concerned about others than himself, even in His agony. His forgiving love embraces us all.

When a thief on an adjacent cross turned to Him, and said, "Jesus, remember me when thou comest unto thy kingdom". Jesus answered him, "Verily I say unto thee, today shall thou be with me in paradise." Jesus was bringing comfort to a sinner. Longinus felt Jesus was speaking to Longinus himself. He would never forget, "Jesus, remember me!"

Even to the end, Jesus cared about other more than himself when he spoke to Mary and John, he had no self-pity. And when He asked God why He was being forsaken, it was, to Longinus, almost as if He was for a moment afraid He had let God down, for, above all, it showed His concern for His God. His relationship with God was by far the most important thing in His life. Longinus understood that so many of us want God for what we can get out of Him. In truth, God wants us for ourselves and we want God for

Himself. Life without God is no life. Not that God forsakes us, but we forsake God.

Not until Jesus had provided for others, did he think of Himself, He thirsted. Longinus learned the meaning of, "It is finished". Jesus had done what was asked of Him. He had given up everything for His God, and He had come to His death rather than recant. It is a cry of triumph. When He commended His spirit to God, the earth shook, bewailing the death of its God.

Longinus pierced that sacred body, and water and blood poured out on to his hands, by which he was united to his Savior. Longinus confessed that those hours by the Cross changed his life completely. There were few who had known the Christ as he had. He sought the Apostles for instruction and baptism and became a soldier of Jesus, instead of Rome.

He could not forget the thief hanging beside Jesus. He asked himself, "What about the outcasts of society?" The penitent thief and, for that matter, the impenitent one? Charity was on Christ's last breath.

"Do I Longinus know what Brother Paul meant by charity, the charity of Christ upon the Cross? "Finally, he asked, "What is my attitude toward men, censorious, or charitable?"

We may reflect with Longinus on our goodwill towards each other. Are we charitable towards our own members or are we judgmental and self-centered? Are we supporting each other the way Christ wanted us to? Do we ever undermine each other? May we remember the fateful watch of a transformed centurion :

Lord, please today send the Holy Spirit and pour into our hearts that most excellent gift of charity so that we may uphold God's work .

Lord, we need your presence in our ministry.

We know the road to peace is filled with rocks and holes.

How can nations and churches travel the road when neighbors find it difficult and brothers often stumble? Help us take the steps to find the way to peace among ourselves for your glory. We pray for the gift of brotherly charity.

百夫長的日記

最近看到一本小冊子，戲劇性地記錄下基督被釘十字架的時候, 一個百夫長的見証。他的所見所聞概括著基督的本質。此文與眾分享的，是傳說中百夫長“朗吉那斯 ”與基督間的親密經驗。

作為負責行刑的百夫長，於耶穌受難的當日，朗吉那斯親耳聽聞了 “十架七言”：

1，父啊，赦免他們，因為他們所做的，他們不知道；

2，我實在告訴你，今天你要同我在樂園裏了；

3，婦人，看你的兒子......看你的母親！

4，我的神，我的神，為什麼離棄我？

5，我渴了；

6，成了；

7，父啊，我把我的靈魂交在你手裏。

雖然“七言”的每一句都可作深入的神學討論，但此文所介紹的，是朗吉那斯本人的生命是如何被這些話改變的。他原以為所有被釘之人都會滿腹牢騷、咒詛、祈求憐憫、甚至會大聲褻瀆。卻從未見過，一個人居然能夠像這位拿撒勒人一般柔和溫文，祂說，“父啊，赦免他們，因為他們所做的，他們不知道。” 這是多麼地不可思議！苦難中的耶穌，對他人的顧念，遠比對自己多的多！祂以寬恕的愛，擁抱著所有的人。

當祂刑架旁的一個罪犯轉向祂，說：“耶穌，當你得國降臨的時候，求你紀念我”。耶穌回答說：“我實在告訴你，今天你要同我在樂園裡了。” 耶穌的安慰即刻臨到這個罪人。而朗吉那斯感到，耶穌當時所說的每一句話其實都是對他說的。他永遠也忘不了那句話：“耶穌，請你紀念我！”

即使到了生命的尾聲，非但沒有自哀自憐，祂還不忘將瑪利亞托付給約翰，對人的關心甚於自己。即使在他喊著說：“我的神，為什麼離棄我？”的時候， 在朗吉那斯看來，處於懼怕的當兒，祂雖然希望上帝介入，但祂不令上帝失望，祂在乎上帝的意願，與上帝的關系超越祂個人的生命。朗吉那斯瞭解，太多的人之所以需要上帝，是因為能夠從上帝那裏得著好處。但事實上，上帝希望我們按自己的本相接納自己，並讓祂的旨意成就在我們身上，這實在是為著人的好處。故此，人要上帝，當單為著上帝自己。沒有上帝的生命，瞭無生趣。不是上帝離棄人，實在是人離棄了上帝。

耶穌為著他人，忘卻自己，直至完成使命，才意識到自己的干渴。以致朗吉那斯開始明瞭，何謂耶穌所說的“成了”。

耶穌成就了上帝在祂生命中的期盼，為了上帝，祂放棄一切，以至於死，且死在十字架上。十架上的話是勝利的吶喊！當祂將靈魂托付上帝的時候，地動山搖，為宇宙之主的死亡而悲鳴。

當朗吉那斯刺穿了那神聖的軀體的時候，水血傾流到他的手中，將他與他的救主從此合而為一。朗吉那斯承認，站在十字架下面的那幾個小時，徹底地改變了他的一生，這個世界幾乎無人如他一般認識基督。此後，他尋求使徒的指示，並接受洗禮，成為基督、而不是羅馬的精兵。他無法忘記掛在耶穌身邊的那個賊，他曾自忖：“那些被社會遺棄的人又將怎樣呢？在這一點上，懺悔的興未懺悔的罪人有什麼不同？噢，唯有耶穌，即使是十架上那最後的一息，所流露的仍舊是祂的慈悲。”

“我，朗吉那斯是否真正瞭解兄弟保羅有關慈悲的教導？是否真正瞭解那出於十字架的恩澤？”最後，他問自己，“我對人又是如何的呢？吹毛求疵？抑或慈悲仁厚？”

如同朗吉那斯一般，我們亦當反省，我們是否興人為善？對自己身邊的人，是悲憫憐惜？還是諸多批評、自以為是？是否因基督彼此相顧？抑或兩面三刀？請勿忘這位被耶穌轉化的百夫長。

The First of the Seven Words

It is widely accepted that there is no atheist in a foxhole. Soldiers in the face of mortal danger learn to pray very quickly. Some say it is an instinct or maybe it is God's presence. Even those who refuse to pray when all seems under control will call out for the unseen when the earth disappears beneath their feet or when the tsunami mounts before them. As a rule, such prayers in the desperate moment are reserved for ourselves, "Lord, save me." It is natural. God invites us to seek His mercy and grace.

On the first Good Friday, Jesus also prayed to God from the Cross, " Father, forgive them, for they know not what they do." Naturally, He would pray in this horrible hour. We would expect any man, even a saint, to ask for rescue or deliverance. But what thrills us is that these first words of prayer were not centered on Jesus himself. He did not ask to be released from the cross. He prayed for his enemies. He prayed for those who tortured Him. His first words hark back to the Sermon on the Mount when He said , "Thou have heard that....., love thy neighbors and hate thine enemy. But I say unto you, Love your enemies.... and pray for them who despitefully use you." He taught forgiveness without reservation. On the Cross, He was practicing what He had preached.

Jesus prayed for the forgiveness of His enemies with complete confidence. He did not say, "if possible". He knew that forgiveness was in His heart. He was not offering extenuating circumstances for those who were killing Him. They knew they were doing wrong. What then was their ignorance? They were ignorant in that though they knew that they were doing wrong, they did not realize the enormity of their guilt.

These first words from the cross may equally apply to us whose sins helped nail Christ to the cross. To receive the forgiveness which Jesus prayed for, we must realize our need, the need for redemption. We must confess our sin. Only those who feel their need of forgiveness will give God a chance. Only those, who know they have sinned, are asking for forgiveness. Only those who tell God, "I have sinned." will share in the first words of Jesus on the cross. Forgiveness is graciously offered to every man, but only those who know they sinned and have come short of repentance will be willing to accept God's offer. Therefore, we should be grateful that the gospels are for sinners, and for sinners only, to help them realize their need for forgiveness. Whenever we feel that our religious life is making us feel that we are superior or more righteous than others, we may be sure that we are not being acted on by God but by the devil. If you feel that you are not conceited, you may very well be conceited.

十架首語

很少有哪個無神論者，或者一個面對死亡的勇士迅即尋求禱告。

有人說禱告是個直覺---事情看起來不錯的時候，人們未必願意禱告，但當遭遇羈絆或海嘯，人們會不由自主的發出呼求---仰望那位不能眼見的至高者。某些緊急時刻，你我都會自然而然的、發出類似的禱告—"主啊，幫助我。"

我們的神，祂希望人願意到祂那裡尋求憐憫與恩惠。

第一個受苦節，在十字架上耶穌同樣向上帝發出呼吁："神啊，赦免他們，因為他們所做的，他們不知道。"在那恐怖、驚懼的一刻，耶穌禱告。

這句話之所以攝人心魄，是耶穌沒有求十字架的解脫，而是為敵人禱告，為那些傷害祂的人禱告。祂的第一句禱告令我們記起登山寶訓的教導："你們聽見有話說，愛你的鄰舍、恨你的仇敵；衹是我告訴你們，要愛你們的仇敵，為那逼迫你們的禱告。"耶穌願人除去仇恨與報復，實施無限的饒恕。加利利山上的祂，親自操練之前祂所教訓別人的話。

耶穌為仇敵禱告，心裏沒有什麼"如果可能"，而是充滿赦免，祂沒有為那些害他的人找尋借口，祂衹是知道，他們所做的，他們不明白，那些人沒有意識到自己的罪孽有多重。

十字架的第一句話意味深長，提醒我們有關赦罪的教導。耶穌為人代禱，讓人看見自己的需要。人人都需要認罪，唯有認罪才能得著被赦免的機會。告訴神："我得罪了你"，才真正有份於祂第一句的禱告。赦免，白白賜下，唯有承認過犯、樂意悔改的人才能得著。

我們因此感恩，因為福音是為罪人、並且唯獨為罪人而設，為喚醒人被赦免的需求。

God, Country, and Our Needs

I received an email with a revealing message about our times. God is not allowed to be mentioned in most public schools anymore. How did we morph from a God-fearing nation of pilgrims to champions of atheism? A new generation has arisen who are ignorant of Bible stories and messages. The email contained a critique and inner expressions from a thoughtful high school student. I am quoting part of his "Poem"---

Now I sit me down in school……

Where praying is against the rule,

For this great nation under

God

Finds mention of Him very odd….

In silence alone we must meditate,

God's name is prohibited by the state.

It's "inappropriate" to teach right from wrong,

We're taught that such "judgments" do not belong….

So, Lord, this silent plea I make:

Should I be shot; My soul please take!

Amen.

It was only two generations ago that the GREATEST GENERATION gave their lives for God and country. Selfless missionaries left our shores to bring God's message to every corner of the earth. Many died martyrs. If we don't see the irony of the times, we may need to be saved in turn by foreign missionaries. Are we going through the typical business cycle of a commercial enterprise, start-up with momentum, growth, maturity, and decline?

How can we, as a Chinese church, become a more effective tool in the hand of the creator? Let us pray for a renewed heart, and a vision with do-able goals. We have to build up our church while our government favors tearing it down. The prophet Haggai said: "Is it a time for you yourselves to be living in your paneled houses, while this house remains in ruins?" (Haggai 1:4) We have to see and take care of the needs of our church----the needs of Sunday School teachers, the needs of the director of youth, the needs of growing in spirit and in finance, and the need of maintaining the house of God….In the Old

Testament, Nehemiah said: "Why is the house of God neglected?"(Nehemiah 13:11) Let us make use of our assets wisely. We need to be better stewards. We need to be unashamedly evangelistic. I invite all of you to offer your thoughts and assistance on the above-mentioned needs.

As God is being displaced in our public institutions, we, as the body of Christ, must redouble our evangelistic efforts to reach those who are godless, who do not know Christ. Now is our chance not only to live our faith, but to share it in a visible way, in their face, so to speak.

The Better Followers of Jesus

上帝、國家、和我們的需要

數日前，有一個全面討論有關時代現象的電子郵件，提及今日許多公立學校禁止人們提及上帝的名字。我們如何能夠由一個朝聖者敬畏神的國家，變成為支持無神論的前鋒？聖經的故事和其中的信息，對新生代來說幾乎如外星人一般陌生。這個電子郵件中有一篇短詩，出自一位頗具思考的中學生之手，抄錄如下：

我在校園坐下，

祈禱在這裡是犯規的，

一個曾隸屬神權之下的偉大國家，

如今提及祂的名字都感到古怪……

靜謐之中，需當默想……

上帝的名字被國家禁止,

是非黑白的教導難合時宜，

人人被告誡不可以界定是與非……

因此，上帝啊，靜靜的，我向你祈求，

如若今日我被槍殺，求接納我的靈魂！

阿門.

僅僅兩代人之前，這個偉大的國家曾經為上帝、為故鄉獻上生命；無私的傳教士離開安逸的故土，將福音傳至世界的每個角落，甚至為主殉道。

如若看不到這一點，今天則成為諷刺，有朝一日，或許要外來傳教士反過來拯救我們。試思想，今天教會是否在經歷一個典型的商業循環----始於沖勁—繼而發展—之后成熟—最終衰退？

作為華人基督徒，如何成為神手中合用的器皿呢？我們需要一個被更新、更信實的心，一個切實可行的方向，　　不可任由教會被荒廢、任人摧毀。先知哈該說：“這殿依然荒涼，你們自己還住天花板的房屋嗎？”（該1:4）基督徒對於福音的需要、神家的需要、人心對福音的渴望當有一個敏感的心。除此之外，教會牧養新生代的需要、靈命和財政增長的需要、甚至聖殿保養的需要……都當是我們的關懷。舊約的日子，尼希米說：“你們為何離棄不顧神的殿呢？”（尼13:11）在一個信心冷漠、是非不辨的時代，求主幫助我們，不以福音為恥，竭盡所能傳揚耶穌的救恩。

Has Technology Outwitted Us?

A scholarly friend recently complained to me that his children cannot read his handwriting and they themselves cannot write. This generation is now enslaved by the keyboard and the screen. In all of Christian history, believers have read scripture and committed many verses to heart, out of love for the word of God. Information technology is so powerful and so portable today, we might have lost the art of memorizing Bible verses. We can retrieve biblical words easily on our electronic devices without much heart or mind. What convenience!

Many adults today can still remember fondly the Sunday Schools where children would take turns writing biblical verses on blackboards and proudly memorizing them. I hope this tradition is alive and well in our church, because no data device can replace our God-inspired brain. The Bible may be stored in our smart phone, but it may not be inscribed in our mind. We have to engrave the words on our hearts. I am not advocating memorizing Bible verses just for the sake of testing our ability to memorize. I strongly believe that we should and can select those verses from the Bible which touch our innermost soul. Each of us resonates to different vibrations. Never let these inspirations fade. Commit them to our heart and allow them to permeate our every thought and deed.

They become the framework of our spiritual being. They are in us, not just in our computers. This is my quest, to share with your one verse or a golden saying as the Chinese say, each month. I urge you to memorize it and live it.

Knowing some Bible verses by heart and reciting them earnestly with heart is not only good for us as a unbroken link to God, it is a wonderful aid in our ministry when those in need find ready comfort in our ability to quote the appropriate words, a timely salve for a hurting soul.

This habit will fill your heart and home with the best thoughts ever written. Let us revive the beautiful art of scripture memory together.

守住我們的傳統

日前與一位朋友閑聊，他抱怨自己的孩子不認得他的手書，甚至孩子自己也不懂得如何書寫。朋友感嘆說，幾乎整整一代的年輕人被鍵盤和螢屏所奴役。他的話頗令人回味。

整個基督教的歷史中，信徒們通常致力讀經，將許多的聖經金句牢記於心，以表達其對 神話語的熱愛。今天，通訊技術發達便捷，不費吹灰之力，我們就可以由網絡上下載所要的任何一段聖經。但是，無意之中，我們也失去了如何記憶並運用聖經話語的藝術。

某個家庭有一隻美麗華貴的花瓶，由祖先傳下，好幾代都端坐於客廳壁爐上的傳家之寶。但是有一天，主人十幾歲的男孩說，這個花瓶被他打碎了。

基督教的文化，和維護這個文化的基本信仰，已經流傳數百代了，從前的基督徒冒著生命的危險將它保持的很好，並且發揚光大。時過境遷，今日卻頗有被失手打掉的危險。我們的輕忽無知、不信軟弱，使基督教的價值備受忽視。若不警醒謹慎，說不定在這一世代中，她會被我們打碎。

要守住我們的傳統，唯有在生活和經驗中去發現和發揚她的寶貴和價值，使它成為活的信仰、活的宗教。如果祗將它當做一件傳家之寶，擺在客廳裡當裝飾品，說不定它真的要被打碎了。

許多人至今仍然能夠清晰地記得，孩童時代於主日學裏，大家輪流在黑板前默寫以及大聲背誦經句的時光。我是多麼地希望這個傳統依舊被我們守住，且運用在我們的教會裏，因為硬盤的存儲是無法取代 神賜予人類的奇妙大腦的。聖經可以存儲在手機中，但它卻無法鑲嵌在我們的大腦和心版裏。神的話需要在心中被融會貫通。我並不認為鼓勵背誦經文是為了一試記性。我堅信，上帝賜人記憶，是為了讓我們將祂那觸動心靈的話牢記於心，成爲生命的祝福，更成為靈命堅實的根基。對上帝的話，人人皆有不同的領受與感悟，不要讓它僅僅存儲在電腦中，任由神的感動褪色，倒要好好把握神的話，記住它、活出它，讓它彌漫在日常的心思與行為上。最終你會發現，神的話不僅要祝福你自己，更要裝備你去祝福那些有需要的人。

讓我們一同恢復這個美好傳統吧！

The Tribes

The organization of the Israelites first took on lasting form when Palestine was conquered. A confederation of twelve tribes took shape with sacral institutions based in faith which preceded the confederation. The traditions had their source in the desert when Moses led the chosen people. Israel's religion was not an abstract proposition, but one based on historical experience. Yahweh, God, had rescued Israel from Egypt and by covenant made them his people.

The covenant was not a negotiated bargain between equals but the people's acceptance of God's terms. It was theocracy with a keen sense of divine purpose. God came again and again to his people in their distress with saving acts which were the basis of Israel's obligation to him. There was no blueprint on how the people should organize themselves in day to day living.

Any member of the chosen people would want to trace his genealogy back to the patriarch Jacob (Israel). Jacob had six sons by his wife Leah (Reuben, Simeon, Levi, Judah, Issachar, Zebulon), two by Leah's slave Zilpah (Gad, Asher), and two by his second wife Rachel (Joseph, Benjamin), and two by Rachel's slave Bilhah (Dan, Naphtali). These were the initial twelve tribes.

The connection between land division and the degrees of kinship is not obvious. The relative standings of the tribes were more or less equal. All contributed to the leadership of Israel. It is interesting that the number, twelve, remained constant while the component members could fluctuate. The major change occurred when Levi ceased to a secular clan and was compensated for by the division of Joseph into Ephraim and Manasseh. Other variations occurred, such as Simeon being absorbed into Judah, but both continued to be counted. Also Manasseh split into eastern and western sections, but the two counted as one, to maintain the number twelve.

The tribes actually absorbed peoples already resident in their territories, so racial purity was not a given. The confederacy of tribes was neither a racial nor a national unit, but a cooperative union in covenant with Yahweh. There was no statehood, no central government, no capital city, no administrative machinery. Each tribe was independent. Each tribe was adjudicated by elders of the clan in accordance with traditional procedure.

The confederation shared a focal point at the shrine which housed the Ark of the Covenant, at first located at Shiloh. In times of danger, there would arise a "judge", a man with the spirit of Yahweh, who would rally the tribes for mutual defense. This kind of leadership is known as Charisma.

This loose government lasted for two hundred years and left lasting effects in the culture of the people. It was the Philistine aggression which necessitated a stronger central government that monarchy came into being. People have argued about the pros and cons of theocracy as contained in the tribal tradition, but many would remember it as the "good old days."

十二支派

以色列人進入迦南後，十二個支派最終成形，宗教祭祀禮儀下各支派間的盟約被確立。宗教祭祀禮儀基於信守盟約，此傳統源於摩西率領以色列民眾出埃及及停留曠野時期。以色列人的宗教並非一個抽象的命題，乃歷史經驗的成果。耶和華神，將他們從埃及拯救出來，又通過盟約的方式將他們歸入自己的名下，作祂的百姓。

這個盟約並非雙方平等洽談訂立的，相反，百姓必須無條件接受 神所設立的條件。這是一個神權管治下，對 神國度渴慕為出發點的盟約。 神一再地將百姓從苦難中救贖出來，是基於他們遵守了與祂的約定。選民生活並沒有可見的藍圖讓他們能夠預先制定計劃。

理論上，所有以色列人都期盼自己的族譜可以追溯到其先祖雅各的譜系中。雅各有六子出於其妻利亞（流便、西緬、利未、猶大、以薩迦、西布倫）；有二子出於其妾悉帕（迦得、亞設）；有二子出於其妻拉結（約瑟、便雅憫）；有二子出於其妾辟拉（但、拿弗他利）。這便是最初的十二支派。

各支派在土地分配和血親關係上的維繫並不明顯，支派間的地位也不平等，但他们均致力於以色列民族的前途。有趣的是，“十二”這個數字始終沒有因為支派間矛盾的變化而發生改變。當中最主要的變化是利未支派從世襲的承襲中脫離出來，而由約瑟和瑪拿西支派代替。另外，西緬支派最終融入猶大支派，瑪拿西支派則分割成為東西兩部分，但這兩部分仍舊歸屬於同一支派，以確保“十二”這個數字的延續。

事實上，由於原住民的加入，十二支派血統的純正必然不如其先祖。各支派間的同盟既非血脈相承，亦非民族聯合，乃是因耶和華神而產生的一個相互協作的聯盟。該同盟沒有獨立國家的地位、中央政權、首府及管理職能；每一個支派各自獨立。各支派內部事務的仲裁亦由支派內長老根據傳統慣例進行。

十二支派同盟的核心關注，則是最初停放於示羅會幕聖壇前的約櫃。在經歷數次危難後，被耶和華的靈所充滿的“士師”興起，帶領眾支派抵禦外族侵犯。

這種鬆散的政權持續了大約兩百年，並在以色列民族的文化中留下了持續的影響。其後由於非利士民族的入侵，迫使一個更強大的中央集權政府產生--君主政權隨之而來。盡管十二支派傳統中　神權管治的利與弊有諸多爭論,但更多的，是對“過往美好歲月”的緬懷。

Root of All Evil

A common maxim is, "Money is the root of all evil." It is so common, it has become a cliché. Cliché or not, is there any truth in it? Many people consider it a biblical quote. If we take it literally, the absence of truth is self-evident. Before money was invented as a medium of exchange or store of value, was there no evil in the world?

Obsession with money or the hoarding of material wealth is actually what the bible objects to... "The love of money is the root of all evil." (1Tim 6:10).

Legend has it that Mammon, a fallen angel, who rebelled against God and was cast out of heaven, symbolizes the lust for money. Jesus said no one can worship the true God and also worship money. Some religious communities try to live literally by this rule by rejecting money. They discourage individual ownership of goods or money. We cannot conclude that evil is absent in such communities. Actually the bible does not denounce wealth. For example, Job was a rich man before his trials and at the end, God restored his wealth. He remained a righteous man throughout. Abraham was celebrated as a rich man. Joseph of Arithmathea who removed Christ's body from the cross was a rich man, a follower of Jesus.

While it is possible to be godly and rich, it may be hard. Jesus claimed that it was easier for a camel to go through the eye of a needle than for a rich person to enter the kingdom of God. Most people value their money and what it buys, more than they value a life of faith. An apt study of the corruption by money is the notorious political hot money game being played in China. It is big money and it is big evil. Money can be corrupting but money is not corrupt in itself. The evil comes when we hoard it; keep it to ourselves, because we love it. This is not only true of the rich. It can be anyone. There are of course many other evils not connected with money, like hate, jealousy, conceit, and meanness to others. Money can do much positive good, like worthy charity and God's work. John Wesley once said humorously that money is like manure, useless if not spread around. Perhaps a better maxim is: The love of money is a root of all kinds of evil, not the root of all evils. I hope we can reflect on our attitude towards money and our duties as stewards in our church.

萬惡之根

有格言道，“金錢是萬惡之源”。這種論調太過普遍，幾乎成了陳詞濫調。但有沒有道理呢？許多人認為這種說法源於聖經。字面上看，其中的道理不言自明。那麼，在金錢成為交換的媒體或價值儲存體之前，世界上難道就沒有罪惡嗎？

其實，對金錢的痴迷，和對財富的囤積，才是聖經譴責的所在。提摩太前書6:10說，“貪財是萬惡之源。”

據說，瑪門是一個墮落的天使，背叛上帝後被逐出天堂，成為金錢欲望的表號。耶穌說，人不能又敬拜神，又敬拜瑪門。有些宗教團體試圖過一種與金錢隔絕的生活，他們不鼓勵個人擁有物質或金錢。然而在這樣的社群裡，但我們不能說，就不存在邪惡。事實上，聖經從來沒有公然譴責財富本身。例如，在約伯受苦之前，他曾經是一個富有的人，而在其受苦之后，神非但恢復了他曾擁有的財富，並令其有所加增。整個過程中，約伯始終持守他的正直。亞伯拉罕也是個富有的人。將基督的身體從十字架上取下來的亞裡瑪瑟的約瑟，是個財主，後來成為耶穌的跟隨者。

虔誠和富有並存不非不可能，但十分不易。耶穌說過，富人進天國，比駱駝穿過針的眼還難。大多數人確實看重金錢及其可交換到的價值，多過看中生命的信念。在中國，如何把玩臭名昭著的政治熱錢的游戲，恰恰反映出金錢所帶來的腐敗，實在是巨富與極惡並存。金錢可以導致腐敗，但金錢本身並不意味著腐敗。若一味的囤積，且嗜財如命，邪惡會隨之而來。這不僅適用於富有的人，乃放之四海而皆准的道理。當然，還有許多其他與金錢似乎無關的罪惡，如仇恨，嫉妒，驕傲，惡意……

金錢同時可以做很多積極的事，例如慈善和上帝的工作。約翰•衛斯理曾經風趣地說，若不四處散播，金錢就會像牛糞一般無用了。或許更妙的格言是：拜金是一種邪惡，卻不是萬惡之根。作為上帝的管家，在金錢方面，甚願我們反思個人的態度與職責。

OFFERTORY PRAYERS

奉獻禱文

Introduction to Offertory Prayers

On any Sunday, many liturgists gloss over the offertory prayer, treating it as a routine, performed almost by rote. This is a waste. We are sometimes guilty of not taking the opportunity of making an impact. One of the important responsibilities of a liturgist is to say the offertory prayer on behalf of the congregation. Too often, this is a bland repetition of some overused expression. Would it not be more stimulating and meaningful if the offertory prayer can jolt us, putting feeling into our offerings to God?

The author has compiled a collection of short offertory prayers to add just a touch of the heart. These are actual prayers used throughout the course of a year. They can be varied to fit the occasion and the church. It is hoped that they are helpful and inspiring in our worship. Let our offertory prayer count and let the congregation take home God's blessing.

[奉獻禱文] 簡介

我們留意到，主日崇拜的奉獻禮儀中，禱文很多時候備受主禮人員忽略，甚至一筆帶過，將奉獻祈禱淪為一種形式，來回重復的僅僅是死記硬背的幾句話。輕忽這個以禱告影響會眾的機會實屬浪費、不當。

教會禮拜中，主禮人員最重要的責任之一，是代表會眾祈禱。然而很多時候，禱告祇是乏味的重複。若奉獻祈禱能夠撞擊人心，奉獻豈不更有意義，更能激勵會眾全心呈獻嗎？

為此作者編輯了這本短篇撞擊心靈的禱文，既適用於教會生活的各種場合，又適合整整一年的主日崇拜。希望此奉獻禱文能夠幫助並啟發我們敬拜的心，唯願我們的禱告觸及會眾心靈，使之滿載神的祝福而歸。

O Lord not in vain, do we make our offering.
We beg you, do not dismiss us,
without blessing us,
without filling our hearts with joy and peace,
without the promise of salvation,
without casting out the fear of death,
without a light in your direction,
without claiming us as your children.
Lord, we only ask for what you will. In your name, we pray.

上主！奉獻不是徒然的。我們不能就此散去----
除非，得著祝福、獲得喜樂、享受平安；
除非，得著拯救之應許、剔除死亡之懼怕，
除非，賜下行路之亮光，稱我眾為你的兒女。
唯上主旨意成全，阿門。

O Lord, we thank thee for loving us for what we are,
even as we are not what we should be.
It is your grace.
We make our offerings, imperfect as we are,
hoping to reach out to you to fill our hearts with
faith, courage, hope, and direction.
We see your face and cast upon you, our every care.
Let your will be done.

上主，感念聖心，納我本相，此乃恩典。
今日奉獻，猶如我眾，瑕疵不全。
今來覲見，求以信心，勇氣，盼望，指引，滿足眾心。
仰望上主榮光，凡我挂慮，全然交托，願主旨成就。

Father, to whom all things belong,
including what we call ours.
We are reminded of your most faithful missionary servants
who glorified you in silence, never asking for donations,
but trusting God to lay it on the hearts of witnesses
to support righteous missions.
Lord, give us the same courage and show us your power to move immovable hearts.
"He is no fool who gives what he cannot keep to gain that which he cannot lose." (Jim Elliot)

父啊，萬物皆由你而來，凡我所有亦屬乎你。
虔誠的傳教士、無聲榮耀你的忠仆，
從未求他人奉獻，卻信任上帝，存見証之心支持公義。
求賜同樣勇氣，賴主能力，改變強項頑固。
聖徒有訓：放下不能持守的，去賺取不能失喪的，
此非愚昧。

O Lord Jesus,
on the cross, you hung stigmatized, and broken for us.
You were offered vinegar for your thirst.
People laughed.
We now kneel before you to admit our complicity
for your necessary crucifixion. Not vinegar, but our hearts.
Accept our offerings and lead us in the way of the cross.
Not requital, only contrition.

哦，主耶穌，
你被懸於十架、受恥辱，為我破碎。
你干渴，有醋奉上，人們哄笑。
如今，我眾跪下，承認罪愆，呈獻吾心，
懇求接納，前導十架之路。
無以為報，唯痛悔之心。

Lord, pour out on us the spirit of understanding and peace. Help us to ask for what pleases you and
when we know your will, give us the determination to do it.
Give us the fortitude of Elijah to say what is right,
and the wisdom of Elisha to ask for the righteous things.
We want to follow your will for our offerings.
Guide us by day with your pillar of cloud and by night
with your pillar of fire. Lead us out of Sinai.

上主，求以了解與和平之靈澆灌，助我所禱得蒙喜悅。
體察天意， 身體力行。
求賜以利亞之堅韌，呼吁正義；
賜以利沙之智慧，追求公平。願此奉獻，滿足天意。
日間，以雲柱帶領；夜間，以火柱引路，
導我步出西奈。

God, you gave your Son to die for us.
They nailed Him to the Cross.
He hung alone that day, to carry all the cost.
He died and then he rose, so all was not lost.
He lives today and watches over us, and for us.
What was our cost? None, whatsoever!
Our offerings can never pay for Calvary,
but countenance us, even for our deficiency.

主，十架之上，聖子被釘，為我犧牲。
祂被挂著，獨自負起所有代價。
祂死而復活，永遠活著，顧念體恤，死亡並不枉然。
我付何價？全無代價！捐獻不足支付各各他。
求勿計缺陷不足，惟聖容光照。

Almighty God, it is never your need,
but that we ask for the privilege to be your stewards.
O Lord, remember not our sins
and never let us be ashamed to wait for thee.
Bless these offerings which are our humble response
to your covenant. Let us also hear what Jesus heard when he came up out of the water of the Jordan---
"with thee I am well pleased".
In your name we pray.

全能之神，非你所需，乃我眾祈求管家之特權。
上主，勿計罪項，勿任憑我眾羞愧枉候,
祝福此響應你盟約、發自謙卑之心的奉獻。
容我眾聽聞天上之聲，恍如出約旦河之耶穌所聞----
"這是我愛子，是我所喜悅的"。
奉聖子之名禱告。

Lord, hear the words of this ancient hymn--
You have come to the lakeshore of Galilee,
looking neither for the wise nor for the wealthy.
You only wanted that we should follow.
You know that we own so little.
In our boat, there is little money and no valuable.
We can only offer our nets and labor, to fish for you.
Fill our nets for your glory.

主，古聖詩說：
你來到加利利湖畔，尋找的，非智者與富者，乃跟隨者。
我們擁有甚少----湖邊船艇，錢囊癟澀，價值無幾；
奉上的，乃漁網、勞力，為你捕撈。
因上主榮耀，請充滿漁網；仆人在此謙恭呈獻。

O Lord, take away our pride and bravado
for we know we are powerless without you.
You are the Master of our fate and Captain of our souls.
Our offerings are in vain if you do not hear the pleas
from our humble hearts, longing to do your will.
Excise from us all traces of personal power, ambition, and pride. Grant us the
wisdom to boast in the pride of
your name, and not in our own arrogance.

哦，主，除去吾眾驕傲、逞能；
除你以外，人無所能。
你乃命運的主人、靈魂的船長。
奉獻純屬枉然，若非垂憐謙卑，渴望奉行上主旨意。
求煉淨我眾，煉淨自我權勢、自大驕傲之痕跡；
求賜下智慧，摒棄一己雄心，唯主名、主榮矜夸。

Our Father, thank you for calling us to be your servant.
Lord God of Hosts, be with us as we affirm once more
our allegiance to your sovereignty.
Grant us the privilege to carry your cross, without boasting.
Let us be faithful to your will, and insist not on our ways.
Fill us with your wisdom so we can be your loyal servants.
If we are right, give us more grace to stay.
If we are wrong, teach our hearts to find a better way.

天上聖父，為呼召我眾成為上主之仆，獻上感恩。
萬軍之主，我眾重申對你主權之效忠，懇求臨格。
賜我權利，負起十架而不矜夸；主旨唯尊，而不偏頗。
以智慧澆奠，信實忠信。
正確的，賜恩助我持守；
謬誤的，指正我心，覓得更美之路。

O Lord, you have freed us from the bondage of sin
and we have chosen to be your servants.
Give us the wisdom to be your faithful stewards,
always witnessing according to your will,
with thoughtful discretion, so that those who have not yet found you will be moved to seek you.
Let us be instruments to guide others
for your name's sake. Our offering is ourselves.
We beg to be accepted.

哦，上主，
釋放我眾，脫離罪惡束縛，成為上主仆人；
賜下智慧，審慎之心，遵守聖旨，作主見証，
成為良善管家；
因你聖名，作合用器皿，使尋而未得者覓得真神。
獻上我身我心，懇求接納。

O heavenly father, spare us from strife.
Forbid that we should judge others,
lest we condemn ourselves.
Keep us on your righteous path, not our own selfish plan. Teach us to be faithful stewards.
If we have walked in our own willful way, please forgive.
Let there be peace in our church, as our offerings
reach your ear in one voice, Hosanna in the highest！

天上聖父，寬恕我眾紛爭。
阻止我眾判斷他人，免得自我定罪；
保守我眾行走義路，不作一己盤算；
教導我眾成為信實忠仆。
若偏行己路，求主赦免。
願教會享平安，同聲奉獻蒙垂聽。和撒那歸至高上主！

O Lord, we don't want to come to you empty handed.
We remember your command to make disciples and to be good stewards.
Let our offerings be pleasing to you
because they come from our hearts.
May our hands never be empty. We ask ourselves,
to whom do we owe the most and who is our most forgiving creditor? There is but one answer, lest we forget.

主，我眾不能空手覲見，
卻紀念上主聖訓，使萬民作門徒、作使徒，
衷心之奉獻得蒙悅納。
主，我眾不能空手覲見，
卻撫心自省：我負何人最多？蒙何人赦免最多？
答案祇有一個，免我心忘記。

O Lord, let us not forget that the small coppers from the poor widow's hand ring the sweetest sounds in heaven. You have commissioned all of us as stewards, one not different from another. We offer to the same Father who hears us with the same ear. Guide us with harmony and humility to serve the same God in one inclusive family of Christ. Our offering has meaning only if we are accepted as children of the one true God, as Jesus promised.

主啊，何曾忘記，
窮寡婦手中之銅錢，曾敲響天庭至美妙音。
你賦予我眾管家之權利，同心向一位父神奉獻，
因上主雙耳，由天垂聽禱聲。
求以和睦謙卑引導，服侍同一真神；
全因被接納，作兒女，奉獻才有意義。

God in Heaven, is it true that the highest suffer the most?
Yes, you were crucified for us.
Let us know that the mark of rank is the capacity for pain.
We seek no power to rule by our will.
Look into our hearts and erase our pride.
Bless our stewardship and help us grow as your disciples.
May our offering be pleasing to you.
Let us know you by sharing your suffering
to become better followers.

天父，苦創最甚者，果真是至高者？
是的！
上主被釘，旨在提醒，地位越高，受苦越多。
求鑒察我心，抹去內在傲慢，不隨己意統治。
奉獻蒙喜悅，成為真門徒；
分擔上主苦難，更多認識、更緊跟隨。

Let us remember the words of St. Francis:
May the Lord make us His instruments of peace.
May He go with us to bring joy where there is sadness;
to bring hope where there is despair;
and to bring faith where there is doubt.
Let us add, may the Lord keep us in His Holy Spirit.
May He bring fruit from our offerings.
May He grant us peace and safe harbor
so we can bring greater harvest to the Lord's house.

謹記聖法蘭西斯的勉詞:
願上主造就我眾，成為和平器皿；
與我同去，憂傷中帶出喜樂；失望中帶出盼望；
懷疑中帶出信心。
惟願上主之靈保守，使所呈所獻結出善果；
又賜平安穩妥之港灣，盛載禾捆歸家。

Our Lord, Jesus.
Let us carry the cross with you to glory everlasting.
Show us the way so we can walk in your steps.
Use our offerings just as we want you to use us.
Remind us to share your blessings and that giving is a privilege. Let us ask ourselves, how much of God's bounty should we keep for ourselves, for we know that
all things belong to God. We are debtors and servants.

哦，主耶穌，容我與你同負苦架，朝向永遠榮耀。
向我展示上主路徑，追隨上主腳蹤。
使用所呈所獻，正如使用我們一般；
藉我頒賜恩福，知曉施予乃權利。
常常自忖，何以持守上主豐富？
萬物皆由祂而來，我眾乃負債者，乃仆人。

Our Lord and our God, look not at our offerings
but into our hearts, just as you regarded the poor widow
at the synagogue. We ask not for one road sign
but endless commands from you.
We need your guidance in oneness of body,
one for all and all for one. It is only wise to give what we cannot keep, and
keep what we cannot lose----
your redemption and promise of salvation.

我主，我神，求勿注目所呈所獻，但求鑒察吾心，
猶如當年會堂的窮寡婦。
不求一次的引導，但求不斷告誡；
帶領教會合一，肢體相顧。智慧地了解，
不能佔有的就當施予，
不當失去的務須把守----
把守上主救贖與救恩的應許。

Lord Jesus, we hear your footstep on the shore of Galilee. We hear the painful steps on the way to Calvary.
And we wait for the glory of the coming of your feet.
Let us trace your footsteps in all our ministry
under the sign of your cross.
We kneel before you with our offerings.
But we remember that "everyone to whom much is given, of him will much be required."

主耶穌，回首加利利湖畔，那是你的聖跡；
各各他山麓，那是你苦痛的步履。
引頸遙望，是那將臨步履的榮耀。
凡我事工，願在十架之下，追逐上主腳蹤。
我眾跪拜、謙恭呈獻，
因為"多給誰，向誰多取。"

Almighty God,
we offer thee so little compared to your boundless grace, but please hear us as we pray in the words of St. Francis of Assisi, "For it is in giving that we receive and it is in pardoning that we are pardoned."
"Grant that we may not seek to be loved as to love."
Remind us that as we pray for others,
others may be praying for us. We are not alone in our prayers and in our offering. We are one in God.

全能上帝，在你豐盛之慈恩裡，今日呈獻微不足道。
求垂聽我眾和應聖法蘭西斯之祈禱：
"在施予中，我們被賜予；饒恕人，我們被赦免；
多尋求愛，少求被愛"；為他人禱求，我眾被紀念；
在禱告奉獻中，在上帝裡，
我眾契合為一，不致孤單。

Heavenly Father, the faithful in years past built your house.
It is our watch, and we stand on the shoulders
of these disciples to see the vision before us.
We are humbled by the Great Commission.
We are awed by the share of burdens to bear.
Your faithfulness gives us strength even as we weary.
Please summon all of us to support our righteous cause.
Give us the courage to not be frightened before the task, but only after!

天上聖父，往昔，上主忠仆奠基聖殿；
如今，我眾一如既往，於眾聖之臂膀上眺望遠像，
又因上主使命，謙卑、戰驚同負一軛。
縱然勞倦，仍賴上主信實，賜下能力。
求招聚仆人，賜予勇氣膽量，支持公義運動，
直到功成。

God, we cannot buy your love with burnt offerings or silver,
but we know that our sins do not stop your love
which is not of yesterday but dates from eternity.
Please counsel us to be faithful housekeepers.
You have shown us love, kindness, and mercy.
You have told us to pass them on because they are not given for us alone.
Your grace is limitless.
Command your stewards. We are waiting.

上主之恩，非燔祭與銀兩得以購買；
永恆之愛，不因人之過犯止息。
求以愛、良善與憐憫教導仆人成為信實管家；
上主慈恩無遠弗屆，教我眾傳遞之，非獨享之。
求主統領，仆人靜候。

Lord, let the tumult and shouting die,
we make our offerings in silence.
Let the captains and the kings depart,
still stands your ancient sacrifice.
What we bring is our humble and contrite heart,
for we know that no earthly offering will suffice.
It is a debt of the souls, which cries to you for forgiveness,
not repayment. Your will, not ours.

上主，願喧囂與吶喊止息，我眾靜靜呈獻；
願統領與王者消逝，依然是十架獻祭。
靈魂之債，地上祭物不能滿足，
今所奉獻，並非償還，乃謙卑痛悔之心。
唯上主旨意成全。

O Merciful God, we love you with our whole heart.
We fear you with our whole being.
We stand before you without a plea, and without defense.
We know you see the spirit behind our offerings,
which cannot reduce our guilt,
for letting your Son hang on the cross.
Only your mercy sustains us, lest we forget.

哦，憐憫之上帝，我們全心愛你，全人敬畏你。
沒有哀求、沒有辯護，因你洞悉眾生靈魂。
聖子被釘，非祭物能消罪咎，全賴憐憫維系，
免得我眾忘記。

Eternal God, we nailed your Son, lashed, spittled,
and stretched Him, limb from limb.
The offering we now bring have no place before the cross. They only tell of our sorrow. We want to share His pain, but too late. We want to escape our guilt, but only your forgiveness can redeem. While our offerings are powerless in the shadow of the cross, where no gain nor loss is accountable, but for our everlasting salvation
and the chains of sin.

永生之神，我們釘死了你的聖子，
鞭打祂，唾棄祂，虐待祂，拉扯祂......
十架之下，今所奉獻了無位置，卻道出我眾悔憾。
欲分擔聖子苦痛，昔為時已晚；
欲擺脫罪咎，全賴救贖赦免。
十架慈恩彰顯的乃永恆救恩，罪惡鎖鏈，非奉獻多寡。

Lord Jesus, you bore our every sin and every weakness on the necessary cross.
Count not our offerings, but hear them in our prayers.
Help us find the compass of our souls
which points at your cross.
You suffered on the cross, from Gethsemane to Calvary,
but our guilt lasts a lifetime.
Guide us to follow the way of the cross
to find peace at last.

主耶穌，唯賴十架，你擔盡我眾罪性與軟弱。
勿計奉獻，求重心禱；助我靈魂覓得朝向十架指南。
十架苦楚，由客席馬尼至各各他山；
我眾負疚，則一生之久 。
懇求引導，追隨苦架，終覓平安路徑。

Lord in Heaven, we know that every moment of union
in your presence, plants something in our souls.
We pray that this moment of our offering
sows affirmative seeds, and that you are pleased.
Nurture us so that we may grow into fruitful harvest.
Always remind us that we depend completely
on your grace, at every moment and for everything.

天上恩主，因你臨在，相聚一刻，成為靈魂撒種之時。
願此堅實種子，由此奉獻一刻撒下，
蒙你滋養哺育，成長至果實累累，得蒙悅納。
每時、每事，全賴上主宏恩。

O Holy One, may we live so that you can use us anywhere, anytime, anyway.
May we work so that you can use us
anywhere, anytime, anyway.
May we pray so that you can use us
anywhere, anytime, anyway.
May our offerings be used as you will, now and here.
Lord, deliver your servants from the arrogance that thinks it knows all things
anywhere, anytime, anyway.

哦，聖潔之主，
無論何時何地，願我眾生活為你所用；
無論何時何地，願我眾工作為你所用；
無論何時何地，願我眾祈禱為你所用。
此時此地，願此奉獻，照你旨意，為你所用。
上主，無論何時何地，
救助仆人遠離傲慢自是、自大、自以為知。

Our God, our Lord, our offering is but one prayer.
Teach us how to pray
so that our utterances will resonate in your infinite realm. You have told us that prayers are the only earthly force that can move the powers of heaven, the hands of God.
We pray for your will to be done,
for we know you grant the best,
to those who leave the choice with you.

我主、我神，奉獻乃是祈禱。
教導我眾禱告，使此禱聲回響於永恆國度。
你曾說，禱告乃地上唯一搖動神手、撼動天庭之力量；
你未曾賜下一樣好處，不給那以你為主之人。
願上主旨意成就。

Lord God of all,
we know giving does not necessitate love,
but love necessitates giving.
We give, not by law, but by love.
Even if we cannot do great things
show us how to do small things with great love.
Bless our offerings this day.
Remind us when we give of ourselves we truly give.

萬有主宰，
施予未必因愛而發，但愛必定施予。
施予非因律法、乃因愛。
即或不能建樹偉業，卻曉諭我眾因大愛從事微小。
祝福今日奉獻，訓誨我眾，真奉獻乃全人呈上。

Loving God,
We want to be the clay in the hands of the eternal potter.
When you answer prayers we will act beyond our words.
Use us today, now. We know that
now is the accepted time to give, not tomorrow,
not some more convenient season. It is today
that our offering can be made, and your appointed work can be done, not some future day or future year.
The crucifixion did not wait for a better day.

全愛之神，
願我成為永恆窯匠手中之泥土，
應允所求，成就大事；
今時此刻，為你所用。
奉獻，非明天、非適宜之季節，
乃今時、此刻得蒙接納;奉獻在此，聖工成就。
十架被釘不曾選擇吉日良辰。

Lord, our Master, you have warned us about
the great Deceiver who leads us away from you.
All that is necessary for the triumph of evil is for believers to do nothing.
In our hearts we know that indifference makes an excuse, but your love finds a way for us.
We offer our love. We may be few in number, but still just because we cannot do everything, we will not refuse to do the something that we can do for your glory.

上主，你曾警戒，
那令人遠離你之惡者之夸勝，
乃信徒無所事事，漠不關心，
但上主之愛另辟蹊徑。
我眾寡少，仍須獻上愛心；
雖非凡事皆能，理當竭盡全力，全因上主榮耀。

Our Father and our Maker, teach us to step out
of our comfort zone to give to others like true missionaries, for we remember
your inspired words,
"Give away your life, you will find life given back"---
given back with bonus and blessing.
Plant the seeds of giving in our lives,
so that we will grow rich in your blessings.
Make us good stewards.

聖父，造物主，求教導我眾步出安樂之所在，
學效傳教士，施予以誠。
啟迪豐盛蒙福之道----"舍棄生命的，必得著生命"。
願施予之種播撒心田，成長豐富，成為良善管家。

Lord, make us instruments of your peace.
Make us preachers of your gospel at all times.
We want to change the world for you,
but we need to change ourselves first.
We offer ourselves to be transformed in your image
so that we can reach others, following your footsteps from Calvary. Help us
live your gospel and preach the Word,
with words when necessary. Because you say so,
we will let down the nets to catch men.

上主，使我成為和平器皿，四周宣揚福音。
為你改變世界，當先改變一己。
學效聖范，獻上全人，關顧大眾，
活出聖訓，傳遞救恩。
起行於加略山，追隨上主腳蹤，
你為此被差，又如此吩咐，使我得人如得魚。

O Lord, show us how to love until it hurts,
then there can be no more hurt, only more love.
Let our offering touch those who are poor in spirit and love.
Our offerings are our invitation for you to please
come into our hearts and give us your gift of eternal life,
while we give of ourselves
in true joy and peace.

哦，上主，愛會受傷，但愛能除去傷害；
願此奉獻觸動人心，填補愛之匱乏。
喜樂平安中，我眾歡然呈獻，
懇請進入吾心，賜下永生。

Our Lord in Heaven, we thank you for the joy of giving
and for the joy that it gives when it brightens the life
of some weary fellow traveler in life.
Remind us that it matters none how long we may live
as long as we live to give in your name.
We are privileged to give, to share another's load, because we have received more
than our share of gifts from you.

天上之主，感謝賜施予之喜樂。
因著施予，疲憊旅者重煥生命光彩。
塵世壽數，無足挂齒，唯因主愛，施予不絕。
蒙主供應，休戚與共。
施予，實乃權利。

O Lord, help us to learn again
that selfishness and happiness can never go together.
Let us bring help and comfort to others.
Give us the wisdom to know when to speak, when to act.
Encourage us to live up to faithful stewardship.
Thank you for the presence of Jesus among us and the friendship we have with you, because of Him.

哦，主，自私與歡樂，道不同，不相為謀。
賜我眾智慧勇氣，傳遞救助與慰藉，
坐言起行，信實服務。
因上主臨格友愛，獻上感恩。
全因耶穌。

O Father, please take from us all envy, and all anger.
Give us the relief from worry and regret
which only you can.
Help us to be at peace with ourselves, at peace with our fellowmen, and, most of all at peace with you.
Tell us that you are pleased with our giving,
but hearten us to offer more from your bounty.

父啊，驅除妒忌與惱怒，
除你以外，無從釋放，無從脫離憂慮懊悔。
助我與己、與人、與你相合。
曉諭我眾，今所呈獻，得蒙悅納；
激勵我眾，因你豐足，奉獻踴躍。

O God, although we are sinners, help us to know and to remember that we are forgiven sinners.
Help us not to worry about tomorrow, but to know that we will not be tried above and beyond what we can bear.
Help us become givers of ourselves so that we will find true joy of heart and peace of mind.

上帝，我皆罪人，卻蒙赦罪。
救助我眾，勿憂未來，謹記試煉必不超越己所能受，
卻將身心獻上，享受喜樂之心，平安之靈。

Lord in Heaven, give us light for our way, strength for our tasks, peace for our worries , and forgiveness for our sins.
Please do not reckon our offerings because we are sure to be found wanting. In no way, are we balancing our spiritual accounts. As your children through Jesus, speak to our minds and hearts so that we may rest our problems in the clasp of your everlasting arms.

天上的恩主，求賜行路之亮光，工作之力量；
平息顧慮，赦免罪愆。
勿計奉獻之多寡，因其不足支付靈之債項；
卻因基督，向吾眾說話，在其永遠之膀臂中，憂慮卸下。

Dear God, breathe into us the kindness,
which will give us a quick eye to see what we can do for others, and a ready hand to do it.
Impart into us the constant awareness of your presence, which makes us do everything as unto you.
Our offerings are but a small tribute to your all-powerful kingdom. Abide us as your loyal stewards.
Teach us to forget ourselves in bringing joy to your household and to beckon to those who have not yet found your house.

親愛的上帝，
求向我吹拂仁慈，洞悉他人所需，並施予援手；
求賜我不斷省悟，明鑒上主臨格，賴主成就萬事。
全能國度中，奉獻微不足道。
容我作你仆役，全然忘我，
攜喜樂入聖殿，吸引未信者覲見。

Almighty God, we thank you for your kindness and grace.
Lead us unto imitations of your Son, the Christ.
Grow our glad and grateful hearts.
Empower us so that we become more fruitful stewards. Grant that today, men may see in us a glimpse of the life of our Blessed Lord.
We know that nothing is ours alone, and sharing is the reflection of our souls.

全能之神，感謝上主慈恩，
助我學效聖范，增長歡樂感恩之心；
賜我力量，結果累累，使人瞥見上主榮光。
我本無所擁屬，分享映襯靈魂。

Our Lord, God, and Eternal Friend,
please hear our prayers not only in times of our need,
but in our every waking hour.
We know that you are not only our rescuer but the Friend with whom we live day by day. Please let us keep this friendship in good repair through our prayers.
Our offering is a prayer of steadfast stewardship.
Spare us from being followers only in crises,
who only awaken to "All's lost! To Prayer! To prayer!"

我主、我神、永恆之友，
求聽我眾祈禱，於需要之時，更於每時每刻。
成為我眾拯救，更作親密良友，
禱告結此情誼，奉獻乃管家之禱告。
跟隨上主，無論危難平安，時時儆醒，禱告不倦。

CHINESE CHRISTIAN THEORIA
Joel Kwok

O Lord, You are the God of all, but you are our Father because of what Jesus was,
because of what He told us, because of what He did.
We therefore feel the confidence, trust, and intimacy
to pray to you as your children.
We bring offerings to you in filial piety and love.
There is no greater happiness
than for you to accept what we bring.

主，你乃萬主之神，又是眾生之父。
因著基督，其所言所行，
我眾得著信心、信賴、親密，
如兒女般祈求，以孝敬愛心奉獻，
此乃無與倫比之喜樂。

Almighty God, all things are possible if you will.
Teach us what to pray for.
You are the searcher of the hearts of men
and you know our deepest being.
Speak to us even as we pray.
It is not our offerings that move your hand
but the righteous supplications.
Our reward is your presence.
Find a place in our hearts and never leave.

全能之神，在你凡事都能，求教我為何而禱；
你鑒察心思意念，洞悉內在本質。
我眾禱時，求你發聲；
非因奉獻，乃公義訴求搖動聖手，
賞賜全因上主臨在。
求居心內，永不離開。

Our Father in heaven,
we are grateful that you bless saints and sinners alike,
for we know we do not deserve the grace
that you so freely give us.
Yet, we return so little to you, to our shame.
In spite of our debt, we find comfort
when you allow us to ask you to bless those in pain,
those who are lonely, those who are sad,
and those who are discouraged.

天上聖父，聖人與罪人，你同樣恩佑，
白白賜恩予如斯罪人。
所獻甚微，羞慚不堪！
求不計債項，允准我眾祝佑
痛苦、孤獨、傷心、氣餒之人，
由此覓得慰藉溫存。

O Lord, forgive us for the good deeds
we did not do and the help we did not give.
Forgive us for the word of praise and the word of thanks
we did not speak.
Forgive us for our lack of courtesy and graciousness
with those around us.
Forgive us for not giving our church the help
and the service that we could well give.
Help us to try harder.

主啊，
饒恕我眾，知善不行，見義不為；
饒恕我眾，麻木不仁，吝嗇贊美；
饒恕我眾，缺乏仁慈，無禮不周；
饒恕我眾，漠視教會需求，麻木不仁。
幫助我眾，盡心竭力，全力以赴。

God, it is tempting for us to make excuses,
to put the blame on others, and to disown any fault.
It is easy to do so, but it would not be the truth.
Help us not to be discouraged
even when our efforts fall short
and our offerings too feeble.
Do not let us give up the battle for goodness
and grant us more strength for tomorrow.

上帝啊，
尋找藉口，嫁禍他人，
拒不認錯，頗具誘惑，
容易做到，了無真實。
助我不氣餒---縱然功虧一簣，奉獻微薄。
求賜明天力量，執意為良善奮鬥。

Lord, in your infinite wisdom,
show us the true perspectives.
Let us know that our lives have been blessed
beyond all prospects.
Forgive us for magnifying our troubles
and for forgetting our blessings.
Let us think more of others
and less of ourselves from today.
Make us proud stewards of your house.

主阿，你以無窮智慧，彰顯真實觀點，
我蒙祝佑，無遠弗屆。
赦免我眾注目困擾，忘卻祝福。
自今以后，少惜自我，多恤眾生。
成為聖殿驕傲管家。

Creator of the universe, we pray for your gift of senses.
A sense of proportion to see what is important
and what is not important.
A sense of responsibility to know the general good.
A sense of spirit to appreciate the feelings of others.
Most of all, foster the sense to recognize your will,
so that we may do nothing to grieve you.

宇宙之創造者，
賜我眾領悟之恩賜，均衡觀察孰重孰輕。
感悟責任，體察眾生，
吃苦耐勞，諒解他人；
賜我眾領悟之恩賜，明鑒上主意志，免上主憂傷

O God, we can hide nothing from you. Search our souls and correct us with the purity, goodness, and truth which you alone can give. Countenance our failures in our spirit.
Regard not our sparing offering.
Help us win the battle with ourselves on the side of righteousness. Teach us to lower ourselves and raise others. Together, let us enthrone Jesus in our hearts.

神啊，在你面前，我眾無可遁匿。
鑒察我靈，以你純潔、良善與真理糾正；
光照我靈失敗，不計奉獻多寡；
自我交戰中，助我贏得正義。
降卑自我，提升他人，基督心中作王。

O Lord, bless us with health
so that each day we can worship you in comfort.
Bless us with your peace in our hearts
so that we can enjoy the fellowship of believers.
Bless us with the beauty of nature
so that we can enjoy the handiwork of our creator.
Bless us with generosity so that we can share all good things with others in being your faithful stewards.

主啊，祝佑我眾，享受康泰，天天於舒適中敬拜。
祝佑我眾, 享受信徒團契，上主平安。
祝佑我眾，享受自然美麗，造物主之傑作。
祝佑我眾，成為上主忠實管家，
存慷慨之心，與人分享美好事物。

Christmas

Heavenly Father, on that Christmas day, Jesus was the Word made flesh, God who chose to be born in obscurity, not as the Messiah ,
but a defenseless baby in a borrowed manger. Yet, the world was forever changed for us. We remember the words of Isaiah, "Arise, shine, for your light has come. The glory of the Lord has risen upon you." Ever since that day, Lord, our blessings have been too numerous, our hearts filled with joy.
Few would know that this Divine Redeemer would pay the punishment for our sins by dying on the cross. Help us put Jesus back into our Christmas today where presents mean the gift of life and faith. We are grateful that this story has become our story as we celebrate the birth of our Lord Jesus.

聖誕節

天上聖父，那個聖誕節，基督道成肉身，選擇誕生於借來的馬槽。
祂進入世界，不像彌賽亞，乃似手無寸鐵的嬰兒，默默無聞！
然而，永遠地，世界被改變。
猶如先知以賽亞的話，“興起，發光，因為你的光已經來到，
耶和華的榮耀發現照耀你。”（賽60:1）
自此開始，我眾蒙福無數，喜悅之情滿溢。
卻鮮於知曉，神聖救主將因我眾之罪，背付十架刑罰。
懇求幫助我們，讓耶穌重回聖誕，
讓祂成為我眾生活與信仰之禮物。
何等感恩，因基督誕生，祂的故事，成為我們的故事。

Friendship Day

Dear Lord, you have blessed us with friends without whom our lives would be insufferable. Friendship is your priceless gift that cannot be bought or sold but its value is greater than gold. Good Lord, thank you for sending friends who are understanding and faithful. The kindness, affection, and sympathy we feel, remind us of your presence. Lord, in your charity, you have given us true sharing and kindred feelings and a union of thoughts. We are grateful.

友情主日

親愛的主，您祝福我們，賜予良友。
沒有朋友，生活將難以忍受。
友誼無價，賽過黃金，友情之禮不能交易，其價至高。
恩主，感謝賜下理解與忠信之朋友；
其恩情、親情、與同情昭示上主臨在。
因你慈悲，朋友得以真實分享、互為相屬，彼此合一。
我眾為此謝恩。

Easter Sunday

We are lifting up our eyes to you, O Lord, as the poets remind us: Have you ever heard God? Have you experienced new hope when you behold leaves budding on a tree? Or seen a timid flower push through the frozen sod? Opening its petaled eyes to God? It is God saying, "Lift up your eyes to me and your heavy heart will sing." For God never sends the Winter without the joy of Spring. Spring sings of the Lord's greatness and speaks of His love and the wonder and glory of the first Easter morn. For He who was born to be crucified, arose from the grave to be glorified.

復活主日

主啊，我眾向你舉目，又蒙詩人提醒：
當樹葉兒萌芽，你是否聽聞上帝之聲？
當一株含羞小花挺出冰凍草皮，向神張開花瓣的眼睛，
你是否經歷嶄新希望？
神對你說，"向山舉目，沉重之心將迸發歌聲。"
祂不會送出冬季而不賜春之喜悅。
春天詠唱上主偉大妙愛，訴說首個復活清晨的奇妙榮耀。
祂為十架而來，墓中復活披戴榮耀。

Pentecost

O Holy Spirit, who dwells in our hearts forever as our counselor, teach us all things even as we mortals cannot hope to understand all things divine. You filled the apostles at Pentecost and they spoke in tongues. We, who were given new life by baptism, speak your truth. Our salvation comes from grace but our every good act is conceived through you. We have been saved through the washing of rebirth and renewal by the Holy Spirit whom God poured out on us through Jesus Christ. We are heirs of eternal life because of you, to devote ourselves to doing what is good. To us, every day is Pentacost, because we have the Holy Ghost in us. In the name of the Father, the Son, and the Holy Spirit, we pray.

聖靈降臨節

哦，居於我心，永為策士之聖靈，
懇求教導萬事，因凡人不能洞悉神聖。
五旬節你充滿使徒說方言，今以洗禮賦予新生，
我眾宣揚真理，救恩因恩典而來，善行由你被構思。
藉著耶穌基督，
我眾被澆灌、得拯救、被更新、
洗禮重生、承受永生、致力良善。
日日皆是五旬節，全因聖靈。
奉父、子、聖靈之名禱告。

New Year

O Lord, The New Year lies before us like a spotless tract of snow. Let us be careful how we tread on it, for every mark will show. Let no footprint be smeared with the sins of our past. Let the new year be a new birth in Christ. Let our souls be like the pristine snow. We stand once more at the end of one year and the beginning of another. We thank you for your blessings and beseech you to continue to grant us hope, faith, and love. Guide us to walk in your way, leaving no prints in time's sand in wayward ways. Give us the time to pray. Grant us the grace, as another year starts to find time to listen to you and do what you most want us to do.

新年

上主，眼前之新年，仿佛一塵不染之雪道，將印記逐一顯呈，
故須謹慎踩踏，勿讓過往罪衍玷污雪中足跡。
在基督裡，新年伴隨新生，唯願我眾靈魂純淨似雪像。
步入歲首年終，感謝上主祝福，續賜希望、信心與愛。
引導我眾，行上主之路，不恣意踐踏時間沙土。
新年伊始，賜下恩惠，惜時祈禱，傾聽恩言，依旨做工。

Father's Day

Our Father in Heaven, we thank you for the fathers you gave us on earth. They care for us and yet seldom express their feelings. They do not boast but always lend a hand when we stumble. They hold us when we are scared. They are patient and strong. Lord, we thank you for their sacrifice. We wish there was a way we could repay them. They will stay in our hearts always.

父親節

天上聖父，感謝賜予地上生父，
關愛有加，卻鮮於表達、甚少誇口。
踽跚之際，援手所在；懼怕之時，忍耐擔當。
為著父親及其犧牲，我眾感恩，並尋覓報恩之路徑。
父親永居心中。

Mother's Day

Lord, we feel your presence when we are touched by selfless, loving mothers who light bright little candles in our hearts each day. Thank you for the love of mothers which no one can explain. How do we measure devotion, sacrifice, patience, forgiveness, and pain? It is a mystery of creation. Even when the heart is breaking, the love does not falter. Bless all the mothers on this day.

母親節

主啊，每逢被無私、關愛、
日日燃亮心中燭光之母親感動之際，
我眾感悟上主臨在，感謝此無可詮釋之愛。
誰能測度奉獻、犧牲、忍耐、寬恕與疼痛？
那是創造之奧秘。
心會破碎，愛不動搖，懇求祝福天下母親。

Thanksgiving Day

Thank you O Lord for the burden that Jesus carried, so that our load seems small. Too often we accept every good gift from God, the giver of them all, without thanks or praise to the Almighty, we are grateful that we receive more than our share. We thank you for the hand that reached out to help us in every woe. We thank you for the miracles we are too blind to see. Hear our every prayer as thanks for Thee, and know our everyday a day of Thanksgiving for your bounty.

感恩節

感謝恩主，因基督負起所有重軛，減輕我之負荷。
曾幾何時，我心忘恩，輕忽全能者之厚禮；
何等恩典，受多於施，蒙上主聖臂施恩，助我出危境。
為禱告蒙應允、隐藏之神蹟、上主之豐富，感恩不絕。

Lily

CHANG STUDIO, changstudio.com

Acknowledgements

Chinese Christian Theoria would not be possible without the translations and contributions of Reverend Grace Song. In truth, Reverend Song deserves co-authorship, yet she has shied away from such recognition. I would nonetheless like to thank her for her tireless and immaculate work.

I wish to express gratitude to Sunny Woan, Esq. for her invaluable input in the publishing process. She found time in her very busy law practice to make the publication of this book possible through her excellent and effective editing and organization, without which this book would not have been completed. Words cannot express my gratitude for her sympathy with this project.

I am also indebted to Miss Susan Hon of Guangzhou, China, who has contributed much to the Chinese text. Miss Hon has been an advocate of this book and her encouragement to me to publish *Chinese Christian Theoria* made the book possible. Miss Hon emphasized the relevance of this book for the Christians in China, especially the younger generation Chinese Christians who may not be as familiar with the brave efforts of missionaries in the 19th and the 20th centuries.

Finally, I thank *you*, dear reader and fellow Christian brothers and sisters, for sharing your time with me. I share this book of my contemplations to unite the Chinese Christian congregation at large and to strengthen our bonds of faith through a manner that transcends space and time. Dear reader, the most heartfelt of my acknowledgements and gratitude is to *you.*

Joel C Kwok

致謝

首先我要說，離開宋靈光牧師的翻譯與貢獻，【中國基督教雜談】將不會完成。事實上，宋牧師當被列為共同作者，但她婉拒此稱謂。對她不懈的工作和鼓勵，本人深表謝意。

在出版過程中温善铃律師為本書提供了無比寶貴的意見，言語無法表達本人的感激之情。在無比繁忙的律師生涯中，她出色有效的編輯與組織技能令本書得以完善。離開温女士的熱情及俠義之心，此書出版無望。

我要感激中國廣州的韓俏文女士於中文潤色方面的意見與貢獻。韓女士一直是此書的鼓吹者，她多番鼓勵我撰寫有關19~20世紀傳教士的文章，強調他們對中國基督徒，尤其是對不瞭解那段歷史的中國年輕人的關聯性及影響力。

最後，我要感謝你，花時間閱讀此書的親愛的讀者及主內兄弟姐妹。願此分享一己思考的書，能夠超越空間與時間，鞏固维係我們的信心，締結華人基督徒的合一。

親愛的讀者，內心深處，我最由衷的感謝，非你莫屬。

郭志豪

About the Author

Joel C. Kwok Ph.D. is a third generation Christian with a science degree from the University of California at Berkeley and a doctorate in Chemistry at the California Institute of Technology. His childhood was spent in Hong Kong during the tumultuous period of the Pacific War. He was uprooted from Hong Kong to Macau, back to Hong Kong, and then to Shanghai, only to be met by the Chinese Civil War.

Emigration to America during the Korean War was another destabilizing event. His parents moved from Los Angeles to the San Francisco Bay Area where he attended Serra, a Catholic private high school.

He divides his time now between California and Hong Kong. In his retirement from management work for a retail organization, he has taught chemistry in colleges in the Bay Area, California. His hobby is reading, writing, and golf.

Dr. Kwok's concern with the Christian faith centers on the union of the mind and the heart. He has been particularly touched by the acts of modern day apostles, exemplified by the China missionaries.

He presently lives in San Francisco, California.

作者簡介

作為第三代基督徒，郭志豪博士畢業於美國加州大學柏克萊分校後，於加州理工學院獲得化學博士學位。香港的童年時代適逢動盪不安的太平洋戰爭，之後他被連根拔起，由香港遷至澳門，重返香港後，再前往上海，不幸在此又遭遇中國內戰。

朝鮮戰爭期間，移民美國對他來說則是另一個極為動蕩的遷移。他的父母由洛杉磯搬至舊金山灣區後，將他安置在聖馬刁一間名曰撒拉的天主教私立中學讀書。

平生分別居住於加利福尼亞州與香港的他，由企業管理工作退休後，周旋於北美不同的大學教授化學。

郭志豪博士喜愛閱讀，寫作，及高爾夫球。他關心並致力於知行合一、心脑并重的基督教信仰。近代宣教使徒的聖范，特別是近代前往中國的海外傳教士，尤其令他感動備至。

目前，他居住於加利福尼亞州舊金山灣區。

NOTES

NOTES

NOTES

NOTES

NOTES

NOTES

NOTES